Eugene Buchanan, Jason Smith & James Weir

I0804025

# ULTIMATE Paddling Adventures

## 100 Epic Experiences with a Paddle

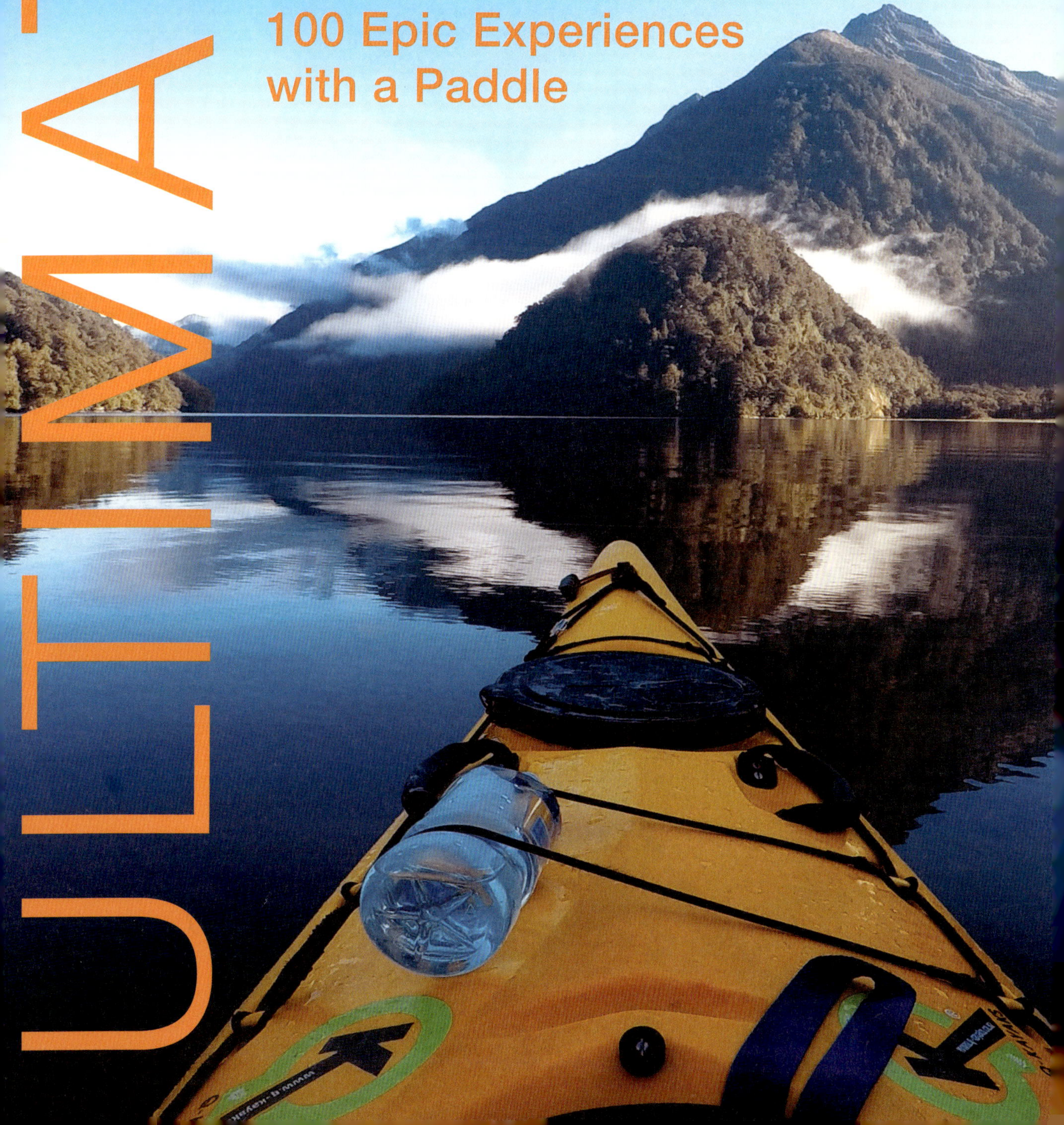

This edition published in 2023 by Fernhurst Books Limited

The Windmill, Mill Lane, Harbury, Leamington Spa, Warwickshire. CV33 9HP, UK
Tel: +44 (0) 1926 337488 | www.fernhurstbooks.com

© 2023 Eugene Buchanan, Jason Smith, James Weir, Andy Burrows, Caroline Dawson, Rob Estivill, Emma Hepplewhite, Chris Scott, James van Drunen

Much of the content was first published in 2011 as *Ultimate Canoe & Kayak Adventures* by John Wiley & Sons Ltd

The right of the authors to be identified as the authors of this work has been asserted in accordance with the Copyright, Designs and Patents Act 1988.

All rights reserved. No part of this publication may be reproduced, stored in a retrieval system or transmitted, in any form or by any means, electronic, mechanical, photocopying, recording, scanning or otherwise, except under the terms of the Copyright, Designs and Patents Act 1988 or under the terms of a licence issued by The Copyright Licensing Agency Ltd, Saffron House, 6-10 Kirby Street, London EC1N 8TS, UK, without the permission in writing of the Publisher.

Designations used by companies to distinguish their products are often claimed as trademarks. All brand names and product names used in this book are trade names, service marks, trademarks or registered trademarks of their respective owners. The Publisher is not associated with any product or vendor mentioned in this book.

This publication is designed to provide accurate and authoritative information in regard to the subject matter covered. It is sold on the understanding that the Publisher is not engaged in rendering professional services. If professional advice or other expert assistance is required, the services of a competent professional should be sought. The Publisher accepts no responsibility for any errors or omissions, or for any accidents or mishaps which may arise from the use of this publication.

A catalogue record for this book is available from the British Library
ISBN 9781912621682

Cover image: www.unsplash.com / Veronique Estie

Designed by Daniel Stephen
Printed in Czech Republic by Finidr

FERNHURST
BOOKS

# AUTHORS & DEDICATIONS


## Eugene Buchanan, Jason Smith & James Weir

**Guest contributors:**
Andy Burrows & James van Drunen (p30 & 48)
Caroline Dawson (p52 & 88)
Rob Estivill (p8, 50 & 102)
Emma Hepplewhite (p80)
Chris Scott (p62, 118)


**Dedications:**

*'To Brooke and Casey. Hopefully you'll get on as many of these waterways and experience as many of these different cultures around the world as I have'* – Eugene

*'For Mum, who passed on to a bigger adventure during the writing of this book, and Faye and Darcy the bedrocks of my life'* – Jason

*'For Zoe, Max and Lilli, I look forward to sharing many ultimate canoe adventures with you together'* – James

# CONTENTS

## Europe



## Africa & Asia



## Australasia & Pacific

## North America



## Central & South America

**Experience**
Novice

**Getting there**
Fly into Bucharest and from there drive 135 miles (217km) to Constanta and another 76 miles (122km) to Tulcea

**In this location**
To canoe the Danube's headwaters like MacGregor did in the Rob Roy, start near the town of Beuron, Germany, and run a shuttle to Sigmaringen (near the Hohenzollern family castle, one of the most powerful dynasties in Germany). Just beware the small weirs, which require portaging or sliding over

**On land**
Take some time out of your boat to explore the nearby town of Constanta, founded by the Greeks in 600 BC and later taken over by the Romans. Highlights: the Orthodox cathedral, Tatar-Turkish Mosque and archaeological museum (with Roman glass from 100 BC)

# RIVER DANUBE, EUROPE

## Paddling across borders – don't forget your passport

Want to paddle the most international river on the planet? J-stroke over to Europe's Danube, whose course runs across, or forms the partial borders of nine countries, including Germany, Austria, Slovakia, Hungary, Croatia, Serbia, Romania, Bulgaria and Ukraine. It also winds through four capitals, including Vienna, Bratislava, Budapest and Belgrade.

If that's not enough to get you packing, set hull to its upper reaches and you'll be retracing the route reflected in one of the earliest books ever covering the sport. The Danube was one of several waterways traversed by John MacGregor, the author of 1866's *A Thousand Miles in the Rob Roy Canoe on Rivers and Lakes of Europe*, and one of his most cherished. Dip a blade in it today, either on its lower delta or upper headwaters, and you'll revisit the waters MacGregor plied in his seven-foot (2.1m), covered, oak canoe, dubbed the *Rob Roy*, with a two-bladed paddle.

When it comes to the Danube, it's easy to see why MacGregor felt compelled to turn his copious notes and insights into a tome. The Danube flows 1,788 miles (2,878km) from its headwater springs in Germany's Black Forest near Donaueschingen all the way to the Black Sea, where it forms the second

largest and best preserved of all of Europe's deltas. In all, the delta at the river's terminus in Ukraine comprises 2,200 square miles (5,700$km^2$) of rivers, canals, marshes, lakes and reed islands, all of which make it a bird watcher's paradise.

Formed around the three main channels of the Danube is its crown jewel: the Danube Delta Biosphere Reserve. The reserve has the third largest biodiversity in the world, exceeded only by Australia's Great Barrier Reef and Ecuador's Galapagos Islands. In all, it contains more than 1,700 plant and 3,450 animal species, including 300 species of birds, many of which migrate annually from as far away as China and Africa. Ply its delta waters in the spring-through-summer bird-watching season and you'll see cormorants, white tailed eagles, pelicans (millions of Egyptian white pelicans arrive annually to raise their young), geese, ibises and more interspersed among such land features as floating reed islands, forests, pastures and dunes.

You can spend as much time as you like exploring its passages, lakes and maze of willow-lined canals. Most paddlers begin their excursions in the Danube Delta by launching out of Tulcea, Romania, about a two-hour drive from Constanta on the west coast of the Black Sea. From here you can paddle such popular waterways as 36 Channel, Sireasa and Papadia canals, and Câslita, Furtuna and Rotundu lakes. Wherever you go, you'll relive what MacGregor noted about the upper Danube all those years ago: 'No river I have seen equals this Danube ... I found it a noble river, steady and swift, as if in the flower of age ...'

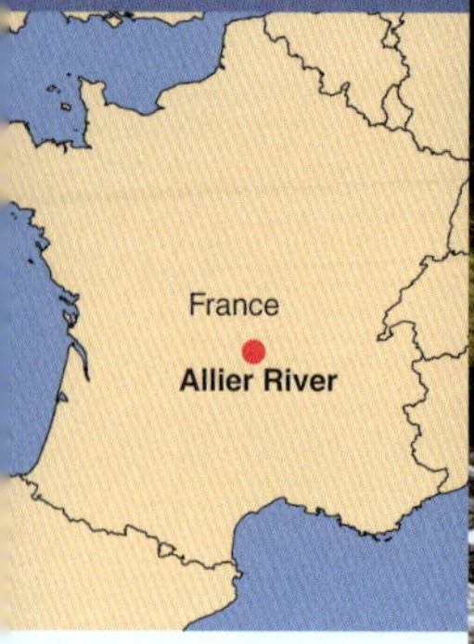


**Experience**
Expert

**Getting There**
Take the train to Langogne, which is on the Nimes – Clermont Ferrand line, approximately 6-7 hours from Paris. If you are going by car you can drive to Langeac and then catch the train up to Langogne with your paddling gear

**In this location**
You can keep going down the Allier if you fancy a longer trip, all the way to Brioud or even further. Expect calmer conditions and more beautiful landscapes

**On Land**
The wild countryside around the gorges is perfect for hiking and biking. The volcanic landscape is dotted with castles and picture-postcard medieval villages that are worth a visit, such as Prades, Pradelles or Lavoûte-Chilhac. Head over to the Puy-en-Vélay for a deeper dive into the region's history and culture

# ALLIER GORGE, FRANCE

## Gorgeous Allier: white water packrafting

This is the longest continuous section of white water that can be paddled in France and has it all: gnarly rapids, extreme isolation, a preserved natural landscape and easy access by train. It is a run made for packrafting. The section here described covers 46 miles (74km) from Langonge to Langeac with an altitude loss of 1,300 feet (400m). The descent can be done in three or four days.

Most of the itinerary is inaccessible by road, with few points of entry along the way. Only the train line follows the natural valley created by the river, tunnelling through the rocky cliffs and crossing the Allier on several magnificent viaducts. If you catch the train before doing the run, it will give you the opportunity to see the rapids from above.

From the train station in Langogne there is a short hike to the put-in. This first section is the most technical and one of the most isolated, starting off with a few class 3 rapids before speeding up to some class 4 drops, the most famous being the Triple Chute. The second part is similar in difficulty with the highlight being the class 4 Freycenet rapid. A few more class 3 rapids will take you all the way to

Chapeauroux and out of the upper section. It is quite long (12 miles [20km] with rapids that need to be scouted) so start early.

The river calms down between Chapeauroux and Alleyras. The scenery is still gorgeous though, with several granite blocks rising out of the water. From Alleyras, keep going into the Poutès reservoir. The dam has been lowered recently to allow salmon to reach the upper part of the river and it is now legal to paddle beneath it. To get around the dam there is a steep path on river left. A carry path should also be built across the dam but was not finished at the time of writing.

The gorge below is the wildest part of the entire trip as the train line no longer follows the river. It often has reduced water levels and is an easy class 3. The water drawn off at Poutès is restored at Monistrol. If you need supplies, here is the place to stop before the classic white water run of the valley, with lots of rafts in summer and nice rapids.

Things quieten down again as you near Prades, a beautiful village with some impressive basalt columns just above the river. Fields start to appear on either side as the river slows down: keep paddling to Langeac.

With stations at Chapeauroux, Alleyras and Monistrol, it is possible to reduce the length or difficulty of the trip. For example, the section between Chapeauroux and Alleyras is a perfect one-day paddle for those who would like to try an easier and shorter version of the gorge.

WHITEWATER

# RIVER GUIL, FRANCE

## Alpine dreaming

The crashing mountain torrents of the French Alps have long exercised a strong pull on kayakers. Its dramatic mountains and challenging and exciting rivers, all within reach of each other, make it a fantastic whitewater destination.

No river in the region offers such a range of experiences along its length as the Guil. A barrage now tames its lower gorge, but the Guil still offers enough action in its upper reaches to keep the most hardened of whitewater addicts satisfied.

The action starts just above the imposing Château Queyras, which sits high above the steep-sided gorge of the same name. This, and the Guardian Angel Gorge, which lies below, are seen as test-piece sections of the Guil and, indeed, as rights of passage to the ranks of the true alpine paddler. Once you enter the Queyras Gorge it's tricky and you need to be on your game. It's very tight and in places the width of the gorge isn't much more than the average kayak's length. In many ways it'll feel a little like being flushed down a U-bend! There's an infamous undercut corner halfway down and care should be exercised, as it is very difficult to protect.

The Guardian Angel Gorge follows fairly swiftly after and the remains of an old road bridge signal the beginning of its challenges. It has many shoots and slides around and over high boulders and also hides some treacherous siphons and undercuts, so treat it with care and respect. It's difficult water throughout and there's one ugly looking drop, in a walled-in section that's impossible to portage and hard to inspect. It all adds to the adventure though and if you take your time, use good judgement and take care, you'll be raving about it in the bar that night. The section finishes where you meet the main road again, close to the L'Ange-Gardien Bridge.

The next section down to Maison du Roy will rank as many paddlers' favourite section of river in the French Alps. It starts with a bang at an impressive series of drops known as Triple Step, which is trickier than it looks as each drop slows you and pushes you to the right and more than one kayaker has taken a rinsing in the bottom hole under the infamous Curtain. From here the section down to the road bridge at La Chapelue is fairly chunky water, with a few drops that call for inspection, and possibly safety cover. Eventually you'll come to a large road tunnel on river right. There used to be a nasty slot rapid here, but flooding has now changed the river's features here considerably. From here it's all excellent read-and-run fun with some good, punchy holes until you get to the take-out at Maison Du Roy, where the river becomes a lake above the barrage.

**Grade**
2-5

**Experience**
Intermediate – Expert

**Getting there**
The Guil is situated in the Hautes-Alpes department of south-eastern France and most paddlers will base themselves in or around the Durance Valley while staying in the region. The nearest airport is at Grenoble

**In this location**
You'll have a plethora of awesome whitewater runs in the vicinity. Fine sport is to be found on the Guisane, the Gyr, the Onde and the Ubaye

**On land**
This is the Alps, so mountain sports rule, mountain biking, gorge walking and rock climbing are all easily accessible. The area also has some stunning Via Ferrata high-level routes if you like heights!

**Grade**
4-5

**Experience**
Expert

**Getting there**
To get to Corsica take either a ferry from the French mainland or fly into any of Corsica's 4 international airports. It's possible to fly to nearby Sardinia and catch a ferry over

**In this location**
Corsica is blessed with a cornucopia of exciting and challenging whitewater rivers. The Fium' Orbo, the Golo and the Taravo all come highly recommended. Its coastline is also considered a world-class sea kayak destination

**On land**
With an impressive range of mountains, over 6.560 feet (2,000m), running down its centre walking, hunting, fishing and mountain biking are all popular pursuits. It's also home to the famous GR20 Grande Randonnée high-level walk, which usually takes 10-12 days to complete

# RIZZANESE RIVER, CORSICA

## Free-falling on the Isle de Corse

Corsica was a groundbreaking destination for early European whitewater kayaking pioneers. They were drawn to its Mediterranean climate, raging torrents and deep, impenetrable canyons. The rivers of Corsica reflect its people, hard, tough and uncompromising. Treat them with respect and they'll offer you a memorable welcome. But slight them at your peril. Of all the fantastic rivers of this granite isle, nowhere is this comparison more true than with the Rizzanese.

The Rizzanese starts with a bang and from the beginning it presents you with drop after drop, building steadily in intensity as you work your way down. Most of its rapids are complicated boulder gardens or slides and it demands focus and commitment. Interspersed amongst these are larger falls, varying in height and difficulty. As the run builds, one rapid flows quickly into the next and you'll become totally immersed in the rhythm of boat scouting, running strong lines and inspecting the next section. The river itself can be so engaging that you have to remind yourself to look up and take in the stunning surroundings. The canyon walls and surrounding hillside are covered in the maquis scrub for which Corsica is famous.

In the middle of the run, and for many the highlight, is a clean 30-foot (9m) waterfall. There's a pool right on the lip, so you can scout your line and there is also a portage option on river left, although this is certainly harder and probably more hazardous than running the fall itself. The traditional line is to run hard right because an old guidebook said there were 'leg-breaking' rocks in the centre and left. But in modern times many paddlers opt for a centre line launching off a natural spout.

Whatever line you choose, as you slide over the lip and see how far away the landing is your heart will be beating hard before you crash down into the foaming pool below. More rapids follow but care should be taken on the very last fall. The river left shoot is walled in, and severely undercut and forms a deadly tow-back in most water levels. A safer option is to run down the right-hand side of this particular drop. All that is left after that is to paddle the now meandering river to the take-out and then head to a local bar to let the adrenaline subside, while you relive the day's adventure over a glass of Corsican wine and a slice of local wild boar sausage.

WHITEWATER

**Grade**
3-4

**Experience**
Intermediate

**Getting there**
Nearest towns are Castellane and Moustiers. You can put in directly at Point Sublime but this involves winding steps. Alternatively you can put in further upstream at Pont de Carajuan. The water levels on the Verdon Grand Canyon are dam controlled and it's important to check whether there is a release or not

**In this location**
It's a fair drive to the paddling centres of the French Alps, but there is nice paddling in the upper sections above Castellane and on the 'pre-canyon' section from Pont de Taloire to Point Sublime

**On land**
In the summer this is a busy tourist destination so there's mountain biking, pony trekking and bungee jumping available

# VERDON GRAND CANYON, FRANCE

## Cave kayaking in the Grand Canyon of Europe

The Verdon Grand Canyon has a remarkable limestone canyon (average depth of 1,640 feet [500m]) with awe-inspiring cliff walls that attract the best rock climbers in the world to test themselves. Far below these intrepid rock jocks, the river snakes its way through some spectacular geology, creating some fantastic, unusual and dangerous rapids.

It may be somewhat smaller than its American cousin in Colorado, but it shares the same grandeur and inaccessibility. Although the rapids on the Verdon are not particularly difficult, once you've passed the entry to the Canyon at Point Sublime you are committed to a long and demanding day.

Due also to its limestone nature, the Canyon is riddled with dangerous siphons. It has claimed many lives over the years and it is a sobering reminder to look up from an eddy above the L'Estellié rapid and see brass plaques fixed to its fearsome limestone walls in memory of those who paid the ultimate price for a mistake on the river.

Apart from its raw beauty, the thing that sets the Verdon apart is the uniqueness of some of its rapids, where you literally paddle underground. The most famous of these is the Styx, which translates as The Gateway to Hell. And it may feel like that as you approach the cave!

The next subterranean experience will be the Chaos de l'Imbut. A tricky rapid, with a very dangerous siphon, that leads down to what appears to be a chasm in the sheer rock for which you are heading. As you enter, the speed of the water drops off, and as your eyes adjust you will feel both trepidation and exhilaration at what is to come. Underneath you the water gurgles and swirls as it flows around and under the rock. After scraping along in darkness punctuated only by small spots of light from the odd hole in the roof you will emerge into a chamber. Now you have to exit your boat and climb out into daylight.

More rapids follow and the Canyon walls can almost feel like they are closing in upon you. Le Rideau (the curtain) is another heart stopper. As you approach it will appear that the whole river is blocked by a massive rock with the river running underneath it. At the last moment you will see a gap on river left where you can put your paddles by your side and use your hands to guide you through.

More quality rapids follow until you finally emerge on to the calm waters of the Pont de Galétas where, if you've made it out before darkness falls, it can be surreal to suddenly find yourselves amongst pedalos and sun worshippers. That pretty much sums up the Verdon Grand Canyon: a surreal, challenging, but very special experience.

**Experience**
Novice

**Getting there**
Fly direct to Crete (3 airports) or fly to Athens and take an overnight ferry to the island

**In this location**
While Crete offers one of the best places to sea kayak, the Greek islands also offer several other paddling options. Try circumnavigating the islands of Mykonos and Delos, whose turquoise seas are home to several water-based wildlife refuges

**On land**
Bring hiking shoes for a walk through the Gorge of Samarian, one of the most popular national parks in all of Greece. Bonus points: touring the Minoan Palace of Phaistōs

# CRETE, GREECE

## Touring the land of ancient Greek gods

You'll be paddling in the wake of such ancient Greek gods as Zeus, Apollo, Artemis, and yes, even Poseidon himself, with a sea kayaking excursion to Crete.

But even in the presence of these deities, it's the area's beauty that truly takes your breath away. With more than 650 miles (1,046km) of glassy, turquoise coastline to explore, Crete, the largest of Greece's islands at 163 miles (262km) long, is as sculpted for sea kayaking as were the marble statues of ancient gods. And sticking out from its precipitous mountains is the island's base rock of limestone, the building block of marble, that makes it such prime paddling.

Rising above the sparkling Libyan Sea, whose infinite shades of blue and green are so clear you can see a hundred feet (31m) down to the bottom, limestone towers and cliffs permeate the rocky, jagged coastline, letting you dart across bays, poke your bow into nooks and crevasses, and even explore the occasional sea cave. A favourite pastime of paddlers in the region is to play Acapulco cliff diver and jump from them into the tranquil waters below. The white cliffs are also interspersed with beaches to lunch and lounge on throughout the day's paddle.

And as well as traversing the lair of ancient gods, paddling around Crete also provides a chance to polish up on more terrestrial history. Famous in mythology as the birthplace of Zeus, the island lies at the crossroads of three continents – Europe, Africa and Asia – making it a true cradle of civilisation. En route, you'll be plying the same waters as the ancient Minoans, who sailed the same sea in the Bronze Age more than 4,000 years ago. Parallelling its coastline, you'll revisit the romping grounds of everyone from the first Stone Age inhabitants in 6000 BC up through the Minoan Bronze and Dorian Iron Ages.

As for the actual paddling, many tourers start in the protected bay at the village of Matala, which lets you explore the ruins of ancient Minoan and Greek palaces, including Knossos, the famous Minoan palace outside Heraklion. You'll also be able to visit ancient Venetian castles and turreted Turkish fortresses, before paddling by the area's famous caves to such other southern coastal towns as Agios Pavlos. There you can visit an eleventh-century chapel built in honour of St Paul before steering your rudder along the coastline to Marmara Beach, the water-access-only town of Loutro and Sweetwater Beach, where you'll find a gurgling freshwater spring.

As for overnighting, you can stay in family-owned inns and seaside tavernas along the way, offering everything from a comfortable bed to home-cooked cuisine and vibrant local wine – courtesy, of course, of Greek god Dionysus.

**Grade**
3-5

**Experience**
Intermediate – Expert

**Getting there**
Dublin has an international airport and 4 ferry routes with connections to England, Wales and France. From Dublin head south out of the city towards the Wicklow Mountains and Laragh

**In this location**
If the rain is falling and the rivers are high then there's some fantastic whitewater sport to be had. Other notable runs include the Dargle, the source of the Liffey and the Upper Liffey

**On land**
The Wicklow Mountains are a magnet for outdoor sports enthusiasts and there are some beautiful lakes dotted throughout the region. Walking, horse riding, mountain biking and field sports are all popular and easily accessible in the region

# ANNAMOE & GLENMACNASS RIVERS, IRELAND

## Combine Dublin's bright lights with Irish whitewater

Although they both rise in the wonderful Wicklow Mountains, and are in reach of the bars, restaurants and other myriad attractions of Dublin, the Annamoe and Glenmacnass are two very different beasts. One's a mellow and fun run with an exciting finale, and the other's a white knuckle, boulder-strewn blast that is quite probably the hardest river that is regularly run in Ireland!

The Annamoe is predominantly a grade 3 run that provides good sport until it reaches the mini-gorge, which heralds the arrival of the 'main event' – Jackson's Falls. The river crashes over a sloping ledge to form a sticky recirculating hole with a powerful back eddy, that's very adept at feeding unfortunate paddlers, boats and various bits of kit back in to the grip of the hole. This has been the venue for a whitewater kayak race in years past and Jackson's draws big crowds eager to see the carnage unfold. In higher water it becomes a big thrashy hole that needs a steady nerve and a strong stroke to punch your way through. There's a second small fall at the end of the gorge and then steps down a gear and the Glenmacnass joins before you reach the take-out ready for a well-earned pint of the black stuff in the nearby Lynham's Hotel.

The Glenmacnass is a very different kettle of fish indeed. Throughout, the run is tight, steep and technical. The pace is fast and the difficulty high and there is always the added hazard of fallen trees. If you can tear your concentration from the screaming river below you, the surrounding woodland scenery is striking. It's very constricted and tight, and many sections are gorged in. Boiling eddy lines and powerful hydraulics litter the run. Your knuckles will be white, but your eyes will be shining as you rocket through Laragh Gorge and arrive at the Soldier's Hole, the adrenaline coursing through your veins! The Glenmacnass then gives you a brief respite as it takes its foot off the gas, just for a while, before going foot to the floor for the final section down to the confluence with the Annamoe.

All that's left to do now is to load up and head off to Dublin in search of stout, song, whiskey and craic to celebrate your Irish river running double.

Dagger

**Experience**
Intermediate – Expert

**Getting there**
From abroad, your best bet is to fly into Dublin, Shannon or Belfast International airport, and plan your logistics from there. If you're coming from the US, it's about a six-hour flight from the East Coast

**In this location**
Are you kidding? If you still want more paddling after circumnavigating Ireland, you're a nut job

**On land**
Take time before, after or even during your circumnavigation, to take in the country's sites, including castles,the Cliffs of Moher, the UNESCO World Heritage Site of Giant's Causeway, the Ring of Kerry, the Rock of Cashel, and, of course, the tour of Irish pubs

# IRISH COAST

## Circumnavigate Ireland by sea kayak

To sea kayak around Ireland you don't have to hallucinate and finish with a 140-mile (225km), 54-straight-hour push. Even though that's what Jeff Allen and Harry Whelan did in 2011 when they set a new record of 25 days, bettering the 20-year-old record of 33 days. The record now stands at 23 days, set by Mick O'Meare in 2015. While some people take a month or two to complete the journey, others take entire summers, paddling when the weather permits and staying put in pubs when it doesn't (which is often).

What most people share when they attempt this journey is the direction. Whether you start from Ardmore, Dublin, Dingle or West Cork, head out clockwise to take best advantage of the prevailing winds. Regardless, be prepared for a haul. The shortest distance around the country is about 1,000 miles (1,609km), but that entails cutting across bays wherever possible and dealing with the ensuing swell, currents, wind chop and exposure. Try to stay close to shore the whole way and you'll easily double the distance. In general, expect the distance to be between 1,000 and 1,200 miles (1,609-1,931km).

No matter your route, you're in for a unique, cockpit-view glimpse of the country, from the beauty of the Donegal coast to the majesty of the Aran Islands. And whether you're travelling solo or tandem, expect plenty of companionship en route. Expect to cavort with dolphins (circumnavigator Jasper Winn shared the waters with a trusty old dolphin named Fungi) and paddle with everything from whales and gannets – a colony of 50,000 of which nest on Little Skellig rock – to even sharks. While most of the latter will be harmless basking sharks, round Brandon Head prepare for the occasional great white – sightings of these toothy behemoths have become more common in the Irish Sea.

Also expect to have close communion with Mother Nature, in the form of rain, wind and cold. Tales abound of winds pinning paddlers down on remote headlands, desolate islands and deserted beaches for days on end. Weather will also affect your crossings. One of the most formidable is the paddle from the Ring of Kerry to Dingle. Another tough spot, where you'll feel the full force of the Atlantic swell, is near Ireland's most northern point, Malin Head. You'll encounter similar exposure rounding the Blaskets.

Thankfully, you can always find willing ears and refuge in local pubs, where locals will ply you with Guinness to hear your tales and might even offer you a warm bed and meal. Just remember: in the end, the trip is no easy feat and you'll likely curse the elements. There's a reason the documentary Allen and Whelan made of their record-setting trip is called *Into the Wind*.

**Experience**
Intermediate – Expert

**Getting there**
Take the train or fly into Naples or Salerno and then bus to the main coastal towns. The nearest train station to the Amalfi coast is Vietri sul Mare-Amalfi, but you'll still need to get a bus to the coast

**In this location**
Head out for the coves and inlets of Cilento and Vallo di Diano national parks for even more Italian touring

**On land**
From Naples, head to Pompeii and Mt Vesuvius, site of the tragic volcanic eruption burying the town of Pompeii and Herculaneum

# AMALFI COAST, ITALY

## A multi-day trip with no need for camping kit

Molto buono. That's what you'll be saying after a delicious pasta supper washed down with wine as you live la dolce vita on a sea kayaking trip along the rugged Amalfi coast of the Sorrentine Peninsula in the Province of Salerno in southern Italy.

Named a UNESCO World Heritage Site for its towering cliffs, serpentine canyons and pristine coastline, you can paddle 25 miles (40km) from Maiori to Positano, stopping to stay in one of 13 municipalities along the way. If your itinerary allows, you can also include a circumnavigation of Capri Island, a resort since the early Roman days.

The beauty of this trip is that you can leave the camping gear at home, staying instead in quaint Italian villas, chalets and B&Bs along the way, packing picnics of fresh Italian bread, wine and cheese for each day's kayak. If you'd rather stop for a cappuccino and dine at a local restaurant, you can do that too at any number of small towns. And don't restrict yourself to wine; the region is also known for its limoncello liqueur.

One popular paddling route starts from the beach in the town of Amalfi and takes you through deep

blue waters along the coast toward Salerno. Stop number one: the town of Minori, where you can visit an authentic villa museum and, if you're lucky, hit the Ravello Music Festival during your stay. Continuing on along the convoluted coastline, you can explore nooks and crannies, cast glances to the towering cliffs or full reach of the Mediterranean Sea, and stop to pull over wherever you please. With 13 towns along the way, you can pull in at a small port town to refuel or for the night. One possible overnight stop is the village of Positano, whose steep streets lead to a perfect viewpoint of the waters you have just paddled.

Towards the end of the stretch you can continue along a more remote section of coastline to Recommone, where you can marvel at ancient towers and explore Turkish ruins. A side-trip from there takes you to the protected Isca Island, where bird and marine life abound, and further on lies Marina de Cantone and the Isle of Capri, which requires crossing the open waters of the Gulf of Naples. Your reward is another night of quaint Italian charm offering views of the entire Amalfi coastline. If you're feeling sociable try to jockey with the commercial rowboats and paddle into the Blue Grotto, a sea cave known for its deep blue reflections thanks to two entrances letting in light (you can also catch a taxi or bus or motorboat there from Marina Grande).

Other island highlights include Marina Piccola (Little Harbour), the Belvedere of Tragara, a high promenade lined with villas, ruins of Imperial Roman villas, and tall limestone crags / sea stacks rising out of the water.

**Experience**
Novice – Expert

**Getting there**
It is possible to drive to the outskirts of Venice, but the easiest ways to arrive are by train or by plane. The Marco Polo International Airport services Venice. The airport is on the mainland; the water taxis or waterbuses to Venice are only a few minutes' walk from the terminals

**In this location**
There's plenty of scope for interesting sea kayaking in this region of Italy. Head south and you enter the waters of the Mediterranean. Head north and the area around Trieste offers opportunities of day and overnight trips

**On land**
There are so many museums, galleries, sites of artistic, architectural, cultural and historic interest and restaurants they could fill a guidebook! Why not take in an opera at Musica A Palazzo or visit the impressive Doge's Palace

# VENICE, ITALY

## A voyage down the Grand Canal

The northern Italian city of Venice has a fair claim as the most spectacular city in the world. A city as flooded with colourful history, breathtaking architecture and amazing art as it is with water. Queen of the Adriatic, City of Water, City of Bridges, City of Canals and The Floating City are just a few of the names that Venice has borne and give a clue to why it is such an unusual, but fantastic, place to explore in a kayak. Venice stretches across 117 small islands in the marshy Venetian Lagoon along the Adriatic Sea. In Venice the boat is everything! Where other cities have cars, buses and roads, Venice has gondolas, spandolo, vaporetti (water-taxis) and canals.

To get around you must either walk or travel by boat, which makes it the only major city in the world that you can explore completely by kayak. The scope for kayak trips is extensive, from exploring the various islands in the lagoon (almost impossible as a normal tourist), or exploring the coastline, to paddling between the ancient walls of the city's buildings, travelling along the Grand Canal and visiting world-famous landmarks such as the Piazza San Marco (St Mark's Square). Sea kayaks make the ideal craft to experience the city. As the hordes of tourists jostle through its narrow, tangled streets, you glide below, the very picture of serenity, as you take in the city's delights from a singularly unique perspective. To walk across the Bridge of Sighs is certainly a special experience but to paddle under it is truly sublime.

It is possible to just rock up and hop on, but the best way to undertake this trip is to book yourself onto a week's tour with one of the operators offering a kayaking Venice experience. Not only will they be able to supply both kayaks and equipment, allowing you the luxury of travelling without the hassle of transporting your own, but their experienced guides know every inch of the city's waterways and are full of local knowledge and history, which makes the experience of kayaking through The Floating City all the richer. Having a guide also makes negotiating the local tides, and more importantly, adhering to the unwritten rules of the waterways, a much easier affair. As if paddling amongst the living history of Venice wasn't enough, if you want an even more intense experience then time your trip to coincide with the world-famous Vogalonga Boat Race, which takes place once a year. The Vogalonga, which translates as 'long row', is a 19-mile (31km) race around Venice. Motorised craft are banned during the race and as over 5,000 competitors, including rowing boats, gondolas and increasingly, kayaks, fill the waterways and lagoon of Venice, a carnival atmosphere drifts across the water and permeates the city. How ever you choose to plan your trip through Venice you're guaranteed a truly unique paddling experience in a truly unique city. Magical.

**Grade**
1-2

**Experience**
Novice – Intermediate

**Getting there**
Drive or fly to Milan, then head with your canoes to Porte Torro and put in just below the weir downstream on the river right

**In this location**
Above Lago Maggiore there is an equally stunning short section of the Ticino to paddle from Cresciano to Arbedo or enjoy a paddle on the Lago Maggiore itself. In Ascona there are many lakeside cafés and ice cream parlours

**On land**
Lago Maggiore is a popular holiday destination and there are numerous walking and biking trails, Pavia has a rich history and a famous old bridge and Ascona has some of the best ice cream in Switzerland!

# TICINO RIVER, ITALY

## Italy's emerald gem – a touring paddler's dream

The Ticino River is a touring paddler's dream, a secret gem hidden away between Lago Maggiore and Pavia in north Italy. The gently flowing emerald green water meanders its way through multiple channels and around small islands. Paddling the Ticino is a real expedition into the wilderness, although just a few hours from Milan. The best put-in is right by the restaurant in Porte Torro, just below the last of the many weirs that slow the flow of water out of the Lago Maggiore. Portaging around the weirs with a canoe and three days' weight of expedition equipment is a pleasure that should be saved until it is unavoidable.

The Ticino has everything a river needs to be special: sandy beaches, palm trees, islands, mountains in the distance and beautiful emerald green water. Setting out into the flow and taking a deep breath of fresh air is the start of three days of relaxing adventures; every paddle stroke and bend in the river bringing a new level of happiness and calmness to the soul. The Ticino is simply a great place to go canoeing, it is ideal for adventurous families who want to introduce young children to the joys of an open canoeing journey, the gently flowing water making daily progress from camp to camp easy.

The magic of fishing for your own dinner – actually catching a fish, preparing it and roasting it over an open fire on your island camp spot and then enjoying that fine taste of really fresh fish; these are experiences that you will cherish for the rest of your life. An open canoe journey is a very environmentally friendly way to explore the watery world we live in; gliding almost silently across the water, no fuel other than muscle power and nothing left behind except ripples in the water.

Seeking a spot to camp out is as much fun as paddling; you need shelter, wood for a fire and flat ground to sleep. Cooking over a wood fire and sleeping under the stars is all part of a canoeing adventure. Wake up, brew up a pot of tea, breakfast and then load the canoes for another day of adventure. An expedition will guarantee some of the most relaxing, rewarding and challenging days of your life; being totally self sufficient and cut off from the world builds a trust and friendship with your fellow paddlers that you just do not experience on your home run or on an afternoon trip to the local play wave.

**Grade**
2-3

**Experience**
Intermediate

**Getting there**
There are direct flights to Montenegro from various European countries. Overland, Montenegro is easily reached from neighbouring countries (Croatia, Serbia, Boznia-Herzegovina) by bus as well as a train service from Serbia. You can hire a car or take a bus to get to Durmitor National Park

**In this location**
There is a wealth of touring possibilities on its beautiful glacial lakes, a stand out being Crno Lake. The coastline also offers superb sea kayaking

**On land**
Hiking and mountaineering in the peaks of Durmitor National Park are popular and mountain biking is also becoming popular with some great trails now opening up

# TARA RIVER GORGE, MONTENEGRO

## The second largest gorge in the world

The small Balkan country of Montenegro enjoys a marriage of majestic Adriatic coastline with a rugged mountain-studded interior cut through with ravines, river gorges and lakes. And it is Montenegro's whitewater mountain rivers that are a major attraction for canoeists and kayakers looking for something a little different.

The country was once part of the former state of Yugoslavia but managed to emerge independent from Serbia and relatively unscathed after the bloody conflict that swept the region in the 1990s.

The lofty peaks of the Durmitor National Park, near the borders with Bosnia and Serbia, is a UNESCO World Heritage Site, and its rugged spires reach up to the sky. But the true jewel in Montenegro's crown lies below, within the limestone walls of the Tara River Gorge.

The UNESCO protection is no surprise because as you travel down its jade green waters, surrounded by dense, ancient forests of black pines, you'll be surrounded by a wealth of rare animals, plants and

insects. In places it really seems like it has never felt the weight of humankind's touch, something rare in itself in these modern times. The Tara River Gorge is the second longest gorge in the world at a length of just under 51 miles (82km); as it slices through the limestone gorge it is 4,265 feet (1,300m) deep at its deepest point. The water is so clean in the Tara that it is common to drink directly from the river! The locals call the Tara 'The Tear of Europe' because it is violent, wild and yet pure and clear as a teardrop.

The river itself is actually fairly mellow in nature and its whitewater sections offer fun sport, ideal for intermediate paddlers as the green water thrashes and crashes through a series of rapids, with plenty of standing waves and holes to play on, with one or two bigger drops to get the adrenaline really flowing. It's the setting that makes this river so very special though, and the feeling of remoteness and wilderness that the majestic gorge instils in all who travel through it will stay with you forever.

It is possible to spend two or three days travelling along the Tara, carrying your kit in your boat or maybe using a raft as support and really taking your time to enjoy this unique and special place, but it is also often done as a single-day trip taking in the best sections of white water. Kayaks and canoes are the ideal craft to travel through this amazing place. And the Tara combines the thrills of running rapids with the tranquillity that comes from travelling through a place of such natural beauty that it'll leave an impression on you as deep as the gorge itself.

**Experience**
Intermediate – Expert
Endurance training is critical as the stages vary in length from 17 to 30 miles (27-48km)

**Getting There**
(if not by car)
Flight to Schipol then 2.5 hours by train to Leeuwarden Station

**In this location**
As well as enjoying the canals of Friesland on a SUP, you can hire a sailing or motorboat to do so too

**On land**
Leeuwarden dates back to 10th Century. Like the other cities on the tour, it has many fascinating historic sights and stories. Try out the famous Dutch cuisine, which is reasonably calorific to fuel you through the many miles to come!

# FRIESLAND, THE NETHERLANDS

## Do the famous Elfstedentocht on a SUP

The Elfstedentocht is a long-distance skating event, past all 11 historical cities in the province of Friesland. There are records of people skating the route in the eighteenth and nineteenth centuries, but the first organised tour was held in 1909. The tour is held at most once a year, only when the natural ice along the entire course is at least six inches (15cm) thick. The Elfstedentocht has been declared to be in danger of 'extinction' due to climate change. In the past 50 years, it has taken place only three times, most recently in 1997.

In 2009 SUPers started using the 137-mile (220km) route across the canals of Friesland and the SUP 11 Cities has almost legendary status amongst competitive European paddlers. Accomplished windsurfer Anna Marie Valeria Reichman fell in love with SUP in Maui and, on returning to her homeland, conceived the ultra-type SUP race along the Elfstedentocht course. Each of the 11 cities is a piece of history in its own right, offering an opportunity for any support team member to enjoy some sightseeing. At the same time, the competitor tackles stages varying in length.

Preparation for such an event is critical. Even the 'light day' entails stages of approximately 18 miles (30km). The water is supposed to be flat, but the wind can play its part in ensuring a tough physical and mental challenge.

The feeling of mutual support to achieve a common goal generates a great atmosphere of camaraderie. The event is very inclusive and accommodates prone paddlers and paddlers with disabilities.

The organisers arrange a boat that follows the race that can be used for competitor accommodation, which is very convenient for anyone unfamiliar with the area.

Competitors suffer a range of emotions throughout the five days. In the beginning, you are incredibly excited. At the end of day 2, you are so tired after completing the first 58 miles (94km) that all you want to do is go to bed for a week. After day 5, the feeling of accomplishment gives you so much energy that you can do it all again. This roller coaster of emotions attracts people to compete year after year.

One tip to look out for is that some of the bridges are quite low. They can end your race prematurely if you don't duck sufficiently!

NSP

**Grade**
2-5

**Experience**
Intermediate - Expert

**Getting there**
Kayaking in Norway is almost impossible without a vehicle, so most people fly to Oslo and hire a car or drive up through Europe

**In this location**
As well as whitewater kayaking, Norway is a premier destination for sea kayakers. Norway's long coastline offers many opportunities for adventures and expeditions

**On land**
Enjoy a special law that permits people to camp anywhere for just 24 hours so long as the camp is a minimum of 420 feet (150m) away from houses or habitation

# VOSS & SJOA, NORWAY

## A Scandinavian wonderland

In the last few decades Norway has rocketed into the top ten destinations worldwide for whitewater kayaking; iconic images of kayakers dropping huge waterfalls and riding endless bedrock slides surrounded by a jaw-dropping landscape have excited paddlers from all over the world to pack their bags and head to Norway. There are two popular kayak hubs, Voss and Sjoa and, for those people who want to beat their own track, there are also vast unexplored areas of northern Norway just waiting for a team of intrepid paddlers to venture up there and claim the first descent.

The rugged terrain of Norway immediately puts you in the mood for a kayaking adventure, driving down long dirt roads, hiking through the forest and eventually arriving at the put-in. Ice cold melt water thundering past you and disappearing over a horizon line sets the pulse racing!

Setting up safety and cameras before the first paddler peels out of the eddy and lines up for the drop, everybody is slightly nervous as they approach: will the line go as planned? Sitting in your boat speeding towards the edge, trying to time your paddle strokes perfectly so the last stroke accelerates off the lip of the drop and sends you and your kayak flying horizontality through the air. Boof!

A perfect flat landing in the chaotic water at the bottom, but don't give up yet, you must paddle to the shore first before you are swept down into the next rapids. High fives all round, everybody is happy and relieved that the jump went according to plan, a first descent, the holy grail of whitewater kayaking, the first person to successfully descend a waterfall, tonight is party night!

Battling through technical rapids, zooming down smooth granite slides and dropping over the edge of enormous waterfalls then wild camping on the river bank and cooking freshly caught fish over a camp fire, these are the things that every kayaker dreams of.

All this and more is waiting for you in Norway, the land of dreams, trolls and endless paddling possibilities.

**Experience**
Novice

**Getting there**
The Masurian Lakeland can be reached by train, bus or car from most Polish cities and by air from abroad. The nearest airport is Olsztyn-Mazury and the main transport hub is in Ełk

**In this location**
Western Poland has hundreds of lakes for canoeing, including Łagów, Chycina, Pszczew and Zbąszyń. For rivers, try the Class 1-2 Drawa in Drawieński National Park. Other options include the Obra River, which offers 103 miles (165km) of Class 1 water, taking you through historic villages and pristine countryside, and the Warta, Poland's third longest river

**On land**
The Masurian Landscape Park includes 11 nature reserves, including Łuknajno Lake, a UNESCO Biosphere Reserve and the Białowieża Forest, which is a breeding ground for bison. The area also offers countless hiking trails

# MASURIAN LAKE DISTRICT, POLAND

## Generous doses of European wilderness

Europeans bill Poland as the continent's answer to Canada's wilderness canoe camping; nowhere is this more true than in the Masurian Lake District in the country's north-east corner. Extending 186 miles (300km) eastwards from the lower Vistula River to the Poland-Lithuania border, the region harbours more than 2,000 lakes in a 20,000 square mile (52,000km$^2$) area. Dotted with ancient hills formed from the moraines of Pleistocene-era glaciers – with many of its lakes owing themselves to dams formed by the same moraines – the area's beauty hasn't escaped the international radar; the district was elected as one of 28 finalists of the New Seven Wonders of Nature, and is known as 'the green lung of Poland.'

The region's lakes – which include Poland's largest lake, Śniardwy – are inter-connected by rivers and historic canals (like the eighteenth-century Masurian Canal, linking the region to the Baltic Sea), forming a web of waterways for paddlers in one of Europe's most extensive lake districts

While this also draws tourists to such resort towns as Giżycko, Mikołajkil and Pisz, its vastness also spells solitude.

Four different paddling trails connect lakes from Giżycko to Węgorzewo and Ruciane-Nida, and from Mikołajkil to Pisz and Ryn, with two more kayaking trails along rivers. The most popular trail is on the Krutynia River, which flows into Masuria Landscape Park. The 63-mile-long (102km) river can be paddled in portions or its week-long entirety.

A good spot to start is on Lampackie Lake in Sorkwity, where you can tour a church built in 1470 and the von Mirbach family palace built in 1850. Indeed, one of the region's appeals is its place in history. In the thirteenth century, the area was part of the state of the Teutonic Knights. Later it became East Prussia and later still, Germany, where, in the Second World War, the area was known as the Wolf's Lair, or Hitler's wartime headquarters. In Sztynort you can also tour a seventeenth-century castle.

The only thing surpassing its historical significance is its beauty. Its clear waters let you stare through lily pads to sand-bottomed river beds, with rich green banks adding to the collage.

After passing through Lampackie and Lampasz lakes, you'll reach a river region called Sobiepanka, with great camps available at Białe Lake in Bieńki. For camping, head to shore or uninhabited islands, or stay at guesthouses in surrounding villages. Later you'll enter the Królewska Sosna nature reserve, which harbours 500-year-old oak trees and ancient pines. The route gets even prettier between Krutyńskie Lake and Ukta (where you can visit an orthodox monastery in Wojnowo), as illustrated by the tourist-filled flat boats piloted by local oarsmen.

**Experience**
Intermediate – Expert

**Getting there**
Get to Irkutsk by train or plane from Moscow. It's then a 45-mile (72km) bus ride to the lake and town of Listvyanka, where you can ferry from Malaya Kurkutskaya Bay to Perevoznaya Bay on the island. From Irkutsk to the island takes about six hours

**In this location**
Head to the Sagan-Zaba cliffs on the lake's west coast just north-east of Cape Krestovskiy in Pribaikalskiy National Park. Its light colours change with the setting sun and it harbours several petroglyphs. Motorboat to the Ushkaniye Islands off Holy Nose peninsula, where you can paddle with nerpas, Baikal's native freshwater seal

**On land**
For a dose of culture, round out your trip with a jaunt east of the lake to Ulan Ude, the capital of the Buryat Republic and home to Russia's most important Buddhist monastery

# LAKE BAIKAL, RUSSIA

## Siberia's 'Sacred Sea' is a true record-breaker

Want superlatives with your sea kayaking? At 25 million years old, Russia's Lake Baikal, the 'Sacred Sea', is the oldest lake in the world, as well as the deepest, with depths of up to a mile (1.6km). Shaped like a crescent moon, its 12,150 square miles (31,500km$^2$) harbour 20 percent of the world's freshwater. And it's all crystal clear, pure and saturated with oxygen.

All this means that it provides great paddling, with more than half of its 1,200 miles (1,931km) of shoreline protected. While more than 30 islands lie scattered around its perimeter, perhaps the best one for paddling around is Olkhon, the lake's biggest. Situated near Baikal's centre just off its western coast, it measures nearly 45 miles (72km) long by 10 miles (16km) wide, offering plenty of room to explore.

Part of Pribaikalskiy National Park, Olkhon marks one of Baikal's most beautiful locations, with a variety of cliffs, beaches, grasses and deciduous forests whose colours change with the seasons. Its name means either 'wooded' or 'dry', both of which describe its surroundings well.

The only inhabited island in the lake, it is populated by an estimated 1,500 native Buryat people. While you can provision here, it's best to bring most of your food supplies from the mainland. And bring

a fishing rod as well; 58 species of fish inhabit the lake, including omul, white-fish, grayling, huchen (salmon trout), sturgeon, golomyanka (Baikal oilfish) and lenok from the salmon family. Most of your paddling will likely occur along the island's west side, where its bays and rocky shoreline are protected and offer broad beaches for landing, and its north side, which offers striking natural rock formations, including Cape Burkhan near Khuzhir, one of the most photographed features on all of Baikal. The island's northern reaches also harbour such natural monuments as Cape Sagan-Khushun, a natural, white marble promontory, and Cape Khoboy. The island's eastern side is more mountainous, without bays, while its southernmost end contains the island's highest point, Zhima, rising nearly 2,684 feet (818m) above Baikal (climb it for sweeping views).

Be prepared for changing seas as well. While the lake's cold surface waters inhibit clouds from forming above the lake, wind and waves are another matter (waves have been measured to reach nearly 13 feet [4m] on the lake). The area between the island and the lake's west coast – known as Maloye Morye, or 'Small Sea' – also creates its own microclimate, and includes the Olkhonskiye Vorota straits, one of the most treacherous places on Baikal.

Still, the summers are usually calm and history is on your side; countless others have survived there before you. Early human camps found at Saraiskiy Bay are estimated to be more than 13,000 years old, and the island harbours nearly 150 archaeological sites, including rock paintings, ancient settlements, camps and burial sites, most of which are protected by the state.

Grade
1-5

Experience
Novice

Getting there
Drive to Bovec or fly and hire a car. Bovec is very tourist-friendly, visit the tourist office for accommodation tips and up-to-date information on the river

In this location
The most paddled tributary of the Soča is the Koritnica, it flows down from the Predel Pass and provides a short but challenging narrow canyon for intermediate paddlers

On land
The area around Bovec has endless possibilities for outdoor enthusiasts; in winter skiing on Mount Kanin and in summer walking, fishing, climbing. Or for those who want a history hit visit some of the museums and battlegrounds from the First World War

# SOČA RIVER, SLOVENIA

## From mild to wild

Slovenia is a very young country, only gaining its independence from the former Yugoslavia in 1991. This breakaway opened up the borders to tourists and adventurous paddlers started to explore this hidden gem. The Soča River is probably the most famous kayaking river in Slovenia and one of the 'must do's' on every European kayaker's list with sections of river to suit every ability.

There are six different sections for kayakers and canoeists to enjoy: steep, tight and technical rapids mixed with open and easy sections. The third gorge, above Čezsoča, is one of the highlights. The river narrows and the rock walls close in from both sides, so the whole volume of the river thunders into a narrow gorge, where a small drop followed by fast flowing and pulsing water challenges the paddler to keep their canoe going straight. The gorge is so narrow you are barely able to turn your canoe sideways. Downstream from the third gorge the Soča relaxes and widens out, making it ideal for beginners and family trips, the stunning surroundings and gently flowing water provides the perfect training ground for those new to the sport or those wishing to enjoy a stress-free paddling journey. From Srpenica the Soča starts to liven up again, sections called the Graveyard and Siphon Canyon will challenge talented paddlers to pick their way safely through the technical boulder parcours and powerful swirling rapids.

The pool drop nature of the Soča, a rapid followed by a section of flat water, makes it an ideal learning environment for paddlers of all abilities; it is relatively easy to rescue a swimming canoeist and their canoe after a capsize. The clear green water allows for easy identification of underwater boulders and speeds up the learning process. The slalom course just downstream of Trnova is a superb testing and training ground for experienced paddlers, with countless lines and variations to enjoy.

Before venturing onto the river, visit the tourist information office in Bovec to buy an access ticket. The local government has invested a lot of time and money in making paddlers welcome, including installing river map signs at every put-in and take-out and maintaining paths to and from the river.

**Experience**
Novice

**Getting there**
The Bakio surf break is on the north coast of Spain about 19 miles (30km) from Bilbao airport and 78 miles (125km) east from Santander ferry port. There are many surf lodges that offer a shuttle service from Bilbao airport or just catch the bus

**In this location**
There are several other surf beaches near by to choose from, Mundaka is probably the most well known, depending on the swell and wind direction. There are of course a few secret spots to check out, hook up with the locals to find the best waves with the shortest line-ups!

**On land**
The Basque country is full of touristy things to do, hiking in the Pyrenees, a city tour in Bilbao or a walk along the coast with a meal of freshly caught fish at a beach restaurant

# BAKIO, SPAIN

## Feel the adrenaline rush as you ride the Atlantic breakers

Bakio is one of the most versatile beach breaks in Europe, some days suitable for beginners in surf school and on other days producing huge, fast, barrelling waves that will test even the world's best surfers to their limits.

The tone of the jet engines changes as the aeroplane starts to descend towards Bilbao airport. Looking out of the window it is possible to see the swell rolling in towards Bakio. Soon you will be on one of those beautiful waves carving your way across the glassy green face. Quick as you can, off the 'plane, impatiently wait for your baggage and kayak to arrive, through customs and into arrivals, look for a taxi or bus and head to the surf lodge. Wind down the windows to breathe in the fresh sea air as the shuttle cruises to the hotel. Nothing else matters now. Check in, throw your bag into your room and get to the beach as quick as you can. Out onto the beach, feeling the sand through toes again, feelings of anticipation and excitement crowding around inside your tummy, surf, surf, surf!

Boardies, rash vest, spray deck, buoyancy aid, helmet, paddle, kayak and run to the water. The salty water rushes up the beach, floating your kayak and carrying you out towards the waves, freedom and surf. Paddling out through the breaking waves looking out back for the perfect first wave, there it is. Setting up to catch the wave looking over your shoulder and starting to paddle, feeling the power of the wave building as it becomes steeper, you and your kayak accelerating across the face, yes! Very little rivals the feeling of surfing a wave, harnessing the incredible power of the ocean, the loud silence of the waves, just you and the water.

The first wave is breaking onto the beach as you head back out for the next, waiting and looking, trying to decode the rhythm of the swell. Watching the locals rip up their home spot fires you up for more – faster waves and bigger tricks. Every wave brings with it a new feeling of ecstasy and excitement, cutting back across the face, digging the sharp rail of the kayak into the green wall of water, zooming along, everything is perfect. Hours fly by like minutes, your arms feel like jelly and the sun is slowly setting, bathing the beach in a warm orange light, time for one last wave. Every muscle aches as you pick up speed to catch the best wave of the day, rocketing across the wave, looking for the sweet spot to set up one big last trick, flying off the lip of the wave and launching into the air! Surfing the wave all the way back to the beach, reflecting on the awesome day and looking forwards to days ahead, just eat, sleep and surf; life doesn't get any better.

Bakio beach on the north coast of Spain is perfectly suited for catching the swell that travels across the Atlantic Ocean, its exposed location generates reliable surf at all tide levels and at all times of year. The gentle waves rolling in under blue sky and warm sunshine provide the perfect conditions to learn surf kayaking, and for experts to test their mettle.

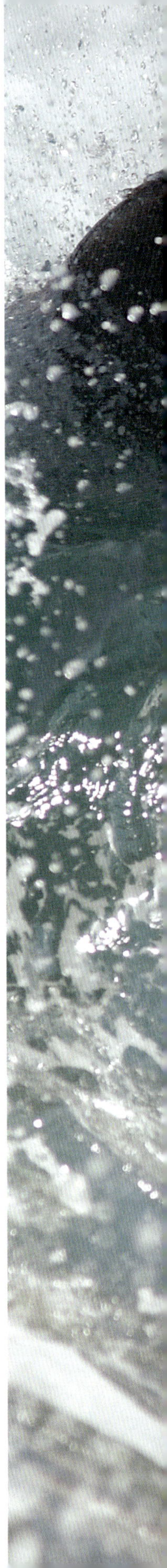

**Experience**
Novice

**Getting there**
Your best bet for accessing Costa Brava is to fly into Barcelona and drive north-east, exiting the town at its northern entrance at Nudo de la Trinidad

**In this location**
Head to the islands of Menorca and Mallorca. In Menorca, paddle from Fornells to Cala Morell. On Mallorca, start and finish from the Playa d'en Repic beach in Puerto Soller and head north-east toward Cala Tuent. Your goal: the island of s'Illeta and its colony of cormorants, as well as the sea cave of Vell Mari

**On land**
Don't spend all your time on the water. Along the Costa Brava, visit famous museums such as the Salvador Dali museum in Figueres, and explore Barcelona's Ramblas while taking in such sights as the Museum of Modern Art and Antoni Gaudi's Sagrada Familia

# COSTA BRAVA, SPAIN

## Sea kayaking the caves of Spain

Spain offers enough sea kayaking to satisfy any adventurer: from Costa Brava, along the mainland coast to the islands of Menorca and Mallorca, all situated in the sparkling Mediterranean Sea. And what it might lack in wilderness and camping options, due to development along the coast, it makes up for in crystalline waters, beautiful rocky coastline and, above all, sea caves.

You can travel the Costa Brava coast from bar to bar, paddling different day trip sections along the way, or try a point-to-point multi-day excursion, linking villages and townships with overnights in quaint hotels. One popular day trip starts out of L'Escala and takes you along a rocky shoreline littered with caves and narrow passages. While the coast is less abrupt here than it is in other regions, lush vegetation and beaches more than make up for any lack in cliffside kayaking. Another popular paddle leads from the town of Tamariu and follows the coast to Cova d'en Gispert, one of the deepest and most spectacular sea caves in the area. Here, you can paddle from bright sunshine into the darkness of a giant

crevasse carved out by Mediterranean surges.

Another day option exists from Platja del Castell (Palamós), whose crystalline waters contrast with towering cliffs indented with small, white sand beaches and coves – providing perfect places to snorkel or rest. From Platja del Castell, you'll follow the coast until Banyera de la Russa, one of the longest stretches of virgin beach along the entire Costa Brava, thanks to local preservation efforts. You'll also get to paddle through la Foradada, a naturally formed tunnel in the sea cliffs: it's easier than it looks; just keep it straight and paddle. From there, you'll reach Cala Marquesa, where the landscape changes from cliffs to more rolling terrain, complete with small creeks that empty into coves with white sand beaches.

If you want a little more adventure, try a five- to six-day trip from France to Spain, starting in Cerbère and ending in Tossa de Mar. Day 1 can take you to overnight accommodations in Llançà; day 2 sees you paddle from Port de la Selva to Port Lligat (where you can paddle around the mesmerising geologic outcrops of the Creus Cape peninsula, one of the largest natural reserves in Catalonia, and visit the El Gigante cave); on days 3 and 4 you can paddle to Roses and L'Escala or Illes Medes; from there it's on to Llafranc, Platja D'Aro and finally Tossa de Mar. You can paddle for as short or as long as you like, picking up accommodation – and, of course, Spanish wine – as you go.

**Experience**
Novice

**Getting there**
The main international airport is in Palma. Many budget airlines fly into Palma from all over Europe. If you are flying in from further afield then you'll probably need to transfer. Hire cars are easy to arrange and the best way of getting around. Some outfitters also offer shuttles negating the need to hire a car

**In this location**
Mallorca has no real inland paddling but its coastline is so diverse and rugged that you'll find more than enough paddling trips to keep you occupied

**On land**
The main holiday resorts south of Palma are where to go if you want to party, but the island has some fantastic castles, cathedrals and places of pilgrimage if you want to soak up a little history and culture. If it's outdoor fun you're after then fishing, mountain biking, hiking and horse riding are popular sports

# MALLORCA, SPAIN

## Set the senses singing amongst the sea caves and coves

Famed as a holiday destination because of its beaches, sunshine and cuisine, the Balearic island of Mallorca offers a fantastic destination for wonderful coastal paddling trips for all levels of experience. There's scope for everything from a relaxing day trip exploring the turquoise waters of secluded coves, bays and sea caves of Mallorca's rugged coastline, to a full-on circumnavigation of the island and everything in between.

The growing popularity of the sport has led to the springing up of several companies offering guided trips or the hire of top quality equipment and kayaks for those who wish to go it alone. This means there's no need to bring your own paddle and boat to the island, which makes for much easier logistics and increases Mallorca's appeal as a destination for a stress-free sea kayaking adventure.

The seas around Mallorca are usually calm and the tidal ranges small, but it can be subject to some strong winds, especially in the north where the cliffs are regularly whipped and buffeted by the infamous Tramontana, a strong northerly wind that can suddenly arrive in every season of the year, except summer (May-August is the best time for kayaking). It is said that whereas you can usually expect gorgeous sunrises in Mallorca, a succession of beautiful sunsets heralds the imminent arrival of the Tramontana.

Paddling around Mallorca can throw up some real contrasts. Cliff-lined sections of coast can suddenly give way to beaches of golden sand! It can be a shock to have spent a few blissful hours paddling along surrounded only by sea birds and your paddling companions to then find yourself landing amongst the deck chairs and overpowering smell of suntan lotion. It is these contrasts that also make it such a different destination for a paddling trip. You get the best of both worlds – the solitude and serenity of the sea enjoyed from a kayak and the lively buzz of busy bars and restaurants bursting with mouth-watering dishes of local seafood. Mind you if you want to avoid the nightlife then there's plenty of scope for wild camping, cooking up a feast on an open fire, watching the phosphorescence glowing in the crystal clear water, sleeping under the stars and so on.

The paddling is as varied and tasty as the food and you'll find everything that a travelling sea kayaker may desire, from the 200-foot (61m) cliffs at Cap de Pera, to the headland of Cap Ferrutx and the sheltered bays and coves near Port de Pollença, where many of the sea kayak operations are based. As you bask in the balmy air of a secluded beach, tucked away in a stunning cove that you have all to yourselves, the smell of sardines cooking on your campfire wafting across the air, already filled with the smell of the sea and the surrounding flora you won't be able to suppress a smile that you decided on booking a beautiful Balearic sea-boating adventure.

**Experience**
Expert

**Getting there**
Fly into Bilbao and then either hire a vehicle and drive or use the cheap and easy bus and train services to get to Mundaka

**In this location**
Many surfers visit as part of a longer surf safari along the Basque region coastline. There's no shortage of world-class waves

**On land**
The town of Gernika was the subject of a painting by Picasso and is a magnet for the region's poets, musicians and artists, so it's a lively and interesting place to spend a few days. The amazing Guggenheim Museum in Bilbao is also a must-see while you're in the region

# MUNDAKA, SPAIN

## Surf boating a Basque Country beauty

Mundaka is infamous in surfing circles and its long, lightning fast waves draw in amateur and professional surfers alike. It's seen many top level surf competitions and has hosted the European and the World Surf Kayak Championships. The Bay of Biscay is a treacherous and tempestuous body of water and as powerful swells crash out from the North Atlantic and onto the craggy coastline of Spain's Basque Country the combination of swell and sandbanks combine in the mouth of the River Gernika at Mundaka to create a break of briny beauty.

On a good day, when the swell and weather conditions align, the wave at Mundaka is a wondrous thing. A steep, angled take-off will lead into the possibility of a 750-foot (228m), or more, screech of a surf kayak ride. It's not for the faint hearted though as all the factors that make Mundaka so great also make it a serious challenge in a surf kayak. Its fame means that when it's firing the line-up will be swamped with visiting and local surfers, all jostling and desperate to catch one of its perilous barrels.

Once you do catch a wave and make the tricky drop-in you'll need all the skill you possess and a seriously fast surf kayak design to be able to cope with the sheer speed with which Mundaka breaks. You'll need to tuck up tight as the wave barrels and pump your kayak's hull like crazy to make the sections and keep ahead of the foaming maelstrom that's exploding just behind your stern, ready to dish out severe punishment should you get it wrong! Catch an edge, or run out of speed and you'll be sucked up, sent over the falls, and slammed into the all-too-close bottom. The only consolation is that it's sand, but be assured that it'll feel more like concrete when the weight of the wave pushes your face into it!

A solid roll, a truckload of surfing experience and a big pair of lungs are all prerequisites of attempting to surf kayak here. Safety is also of utmost importance and you need to be aware and confident in your abilities.

As you scream along with your tendons pinging, synapses firing and hull zinging you'd be forgiven for thinking you'll never make it, such is the length of this Basque beauty. But as you fire out the end of the spitting barrel after the surf of your life you'll be shaking from the adrenaline of it all, and desperate to hitch a ride on the handy rip tide, courtesy of the river, to attempt to do it all over again, pumped up and satisfied that this is one wave that lives up to its hyperbole and well-deserved worldwide reputation.

Lobster Bob

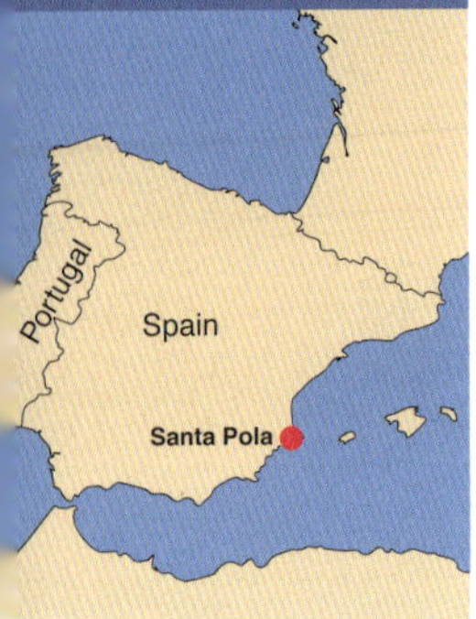


**Experience**
Intermediate – Expert

**Getting there**
Flights are very regular to Alicante airport. Santa Pola is a 15-minute taxi ride from there

**In this location**
Santa Pola offers all sorts of watersports with local clubs offering hire and tution

**On land**
Historic castle and Salt museum. Great pizza restautrants and bars on every street corner. A choice of at least 4 beaches.
A vistit to Alicante is very easy and well worth it. Famed for its beaches, castle, marinas and fantastic tapas bars!

# SANTA POLA, SPAIN

## A World SUP festival for all abilities

Santa Pola is a historic town situated close to the spectacular Spanish city of Alicante. Its beaches face Tarbaca, an island famed for hosting the Barbary pirates in times gone by. Between them lies a stretch of the Mediterranean that can serve a variety of challenges to paddleboarders of any ability.

This is the location of what has become the 'biggest' SUP race in the world. 'Biggest' is described here as the race with the most extensive collection of the world's best paddleboarders competing together. But it is more than just a race of the elite. As its name suggests, it has become a SUP festival available to any paddler to participate in.

There are races to suit any ability and experience. These vary in length and technicality, and the organisers will adjust the course to meet the day's conditions. The main race is a fascinating challenge. Competitors assemble in the early morning to take a ferry to the picturesque island of Tarbaca. The excitement builds as they disembark and search for their race board amongst the 200 or so dropped off at the water's edge.

The race itself is unique. It starts by circumnavigating the island, whose turquoise waters are never still and where the wind always blows. The draft trains are long – really long, and it becomes a strategic journey of hopping between fellow competitors to shelter from the headwinds and save some precious energy for what is to come.

When they reach the large rusty metal buoy, they turn and head for home. This is usually an exciting 6-mile (10km) downwinder. But currents can often complicate things, and the Tarbac ferries go past regularly, creating big swells that can help or hinder the return. The field often splits at this point, and the race becomes a solitary mental challenge. Go too fast, too early, and the racer will not have the energy to sustain themselves.

At the finish, competitors are greeted by a large crowd, upbeat music and a great feeling of achievement. What's more, the set-up is such that there is a SUP village full of equipment retailers, food vendors and a stage that hosts live music long into the night.

Everyone speaks to everyone, making it an inclusive event – a true celebration of the sport.

The World SUP festival captures so much that is good about SUP racing: challenge, competition, celebration and support. Anyone who enjoys racing should build it into their diary!

PACKRAFT

**Experience**
Intermediate

**Getting there**
Abisko is on the train line from Stockolm to Narvik. There are several commercial airports such as Narvik or Kiruna in the region and there are also bus services between Kiruna and Abisko

**In this location**
The Kungsleden and other hiking paths open up an infinite number of possible itineraries both on lakes and rivers. If you head over to Norway, try a short paddle on one of the protected fjords!

**On land**
This is the land of Sami culture, the local population of reindeer herders. Buy some Duodji, handcrafted items made from local materials such as birch bark and reindeer horn. If you visit in autumn, you can try to catch a glimpse of the northern lights!

# KUNGSLEDEN, SWEDEN

## Packrafting the king's trail through Lapland

The Kungsleden, meaning king's trail is a 250-mile (400km) path that cuts across some of the most stunning landscape in northern Sweden. It climbs into the wild mountains of Lapland and connects Hemavan in the south to Abisko in the north. It traverses four national parks: Abisko, Stora Sjöfallet, Sarek and Pieljekaise. The terrain is wild and is criss-crossed with streams, rivers, bogs and lakes.

The well-kept tourist path will give you a relatively fast access to the mountains, with plank sections and small bridges making it easier to cover the difficult terrain and reach the higher valleys and lakes. This opens up an infinite number of possibilities for packrafting adventures. The trail runs in a general north-south direction, whereas the mountain valleys and lakes are often perpendicular. This means you can hike to a lake, paddle down it before hiking over to the parallel valley and packraft back to the main path. There are lots of smaller (and harder) hiking tracks that give the possibility of joining up multiple lakes and rivers. By staying on calm water and using the right equipment, even novice paddlers can find interesting traverses.

One simple loop is to start in Abisko, at the northern edge. It is easily accessed by road and connected by train to both Norway and the rest of Sweden. The Abisko National Park is breathtaking especially in

early autumn when the colours begin to change. The path climbs through the park, gaining altitude and arriving at a first set of mountain lakes, where the run-off from the snow melt gives them a silty blue colour. From here it is possible to paddle south-east down the valley.

The lakes become a small river with several rapids that can be portaged. An almost invisible path cuts through the forests and bogs to the next body of water: Rautasjaure (see picture). This valley is wild, has some stunning beaches and a great view of the mountains behind. Keep an eye open for elk or even bears on the banks. From the end of the lake, it is possible to continue along the river (small rapids, class 3) or hike across the hills back to the main road, where a regular bus service can take you to your next destination. This should take five or seven days depending on the paddling / hiking ratio and physical fitness.

Overnight camping is allowed almost everywhere except inside the national parks and close to homes. There are several cabins on the Kungsleden that are run by the national tourist board, and can be reserved in advance. They can be very useful if the weather takes a turn for the worse.

Remember to pack warm, waterproof clothes, especially good boots and trousers as you will often be wading through marshy terrain, especially on the less trodden trails. Water temperatures are cold even in summer, so carry appropriate gear for paddling too, such as a compact drysuit. To save weight you can use a two-seater boat, that is lighter and faster on calm water. If you visit during the summer months take the time to look for berries: they are a welcome and tasty supplement for breakfast. These include the ever-present blueberries and the harder-to-find cloudberries!

**Experience**
Intermediate +

**Getting there**
Norrköping is a city with excellent transport links in the eastern province of Östergötland, approximately 100 miles (160km) south-west of Stockholm (International hub). To reach Tyrislöt (small waterside car park) will take approximately 1 hour (37 miles/59km) by car, buses only go as far as Sankt Anna

**In this location**
The archipelago is described as 'kayak paradise' so there are plenty of opportunities to paddle a boat here

**On land**
Alnholm Nature Reserve; view rock formations and a giant kettle hole from the last ice age. The reserve is also a haven for birds such as Mute Swans and Eiders. Archipelago Museum is a great day out; learn about how the island inhabitants used to live and their traditions

# SANKT ANNA ARCHIPELAGO, SWEDEN

## SUP and sleep in the King of Sweden's bed

Stand up paddling in the Sankt Anna Archipelago, on the Baltic coast of Sweden is not too dissimilar to paddling in a large lake instead of the open sea. There are no tides, currents or big swells to worry about and when the winds do whip up you can easily find some island shelter to break up the chop.

There are thousands of granite islands to explore by SUP in the archipelago, but there is one unassuming island located on the far outer edge that must be visited. Melskär with its exclusive hunting lodge is owned by the current King of Sweden, Carl XVI Gustaf, it was gifted to him as a fiftieth birthday present by the Swedish military.

The quintessential 'Swedish' red hunting lodge, that sits prominently in the centre of the rocky island, was built over 100 years ago. The interior is not exactly royal standard, instead it is simply furnished with a handmade wooden bed, a small fold-down table and a couple of rickety chairs, plus a fireplace adorned with traditional hunting tools and axes. Outside there is a composting 'King's throne' toilet, a

sawhorse and a rather grand outdoor cooking grill.

It is completely free to use and stay in the King's lodge, but you do need to book in advance. You are required to contact the county administrative board (Länsstyrelsen) in Östergötland to ask if it is available on the days you intend to visit. They will share with you details of where the 'secret' key to access the lodge is hidden on the island.

To SUP to Melskär it is best to park and launch from the small village of Tyrislöt, where it is then approximately a 9-mile (15km) paddle depending on the route you decide to follow through the maze of over 6,000 mostly uninhabited, tiny islands. Make sure you plan your journey well and be confident with paddling on bearings for set distances, the many islands have very few distinguishing landmarks which can at times make many small islands look like one large land mass. Also carefully consider the amount of water you need to carry, as water on the islands can be very scarce, particularly on the outer edge of the archipelago.

You are permitted to wild camp on almost all of the islands within the archipelago, subject to bird breeding restrictions. The islands and surrounding brackish waters are highly protected and rich in wildlife, expect regular sightings of white tailed sea eagles, grey seals and grass snakes.

**Grade**
3-5

**Experience**
Intermediate – Expert

**Getting there**
Tessin is on the south side of the Alps in Switzerland. Either fly to Milan and drive north or drive over the San Bernardino or St Gottard passes

**In this location**
There are a few other paddling areas within several hours' drive from Tessin; Corsica, Piermont or Graubünden, each one full of superb paddling opportunities

**On land**
There are loads of touristy things to do in Tessin, visit the Verzasca dam where the bungee jump from the James Bond film *Goldeneye* was filmed or eat a home-made ice cream by the lake in Ascona. Take a walk along one of the many well signposted paths, explore a mountain village or simply lie back, take a deep breath of fresh air and relax

# TESSIN, SWITZERLAND

## Swiss spectacular

The Swiss canton of Tessin offers whitewater kayakers something very special, bedrock creeks and rivers with clear blue water, smooth slides and wonderful waterfalls surrounded by stunning mountain views and lush plant life, finished off with a wood oven pizza in the evening. Tessin is paddling paradise.

Cruising over the Alps and heading south, a car full of friends and boats on the roof, it is time for Tessin. The sky is blue and the sun is shining, the snow is melting and filling the bedrock creeks that epitomise paddling in Tessin with ice cold water. A feeling of euphoria mixes with adrenaline, boofing the first small drop, rock spinning the rounded boulders and grinning from ear to ear. This is living!

Suddenly the gradient increases and the river narrows, pulses quicken and muscles tense. The water is forced between two big boulders and disappears into a deep blue pool. The first brave kayaker peels out of the eddy and powers towards the lip, the kayak rides up over the foam pile and flies through the air, the deep pool is a perfect landing spot with plenty of aerated water at the bottom of the drop. River water hurtles along at breakneck speed over rocks and round blind corners; climbing over slippery rocks to inspect the crux rapid starts to sap energy, the line is complex but it goes. Safety is set and the camera is running. The paddle strokes must be placed just right, each one using the power of the water to guide the kayak and its rider through the boulder-choked canyon, the water boils with fury as it tries to push the kayaker off balance. Suddenly calm opens out and the rapid is at an end, a fist punches the air and a loud cry echoes off the canyon walls.

The river is not yet at an end as the sun slips out of view. Cold and shade fill the once warm and sunny space between the canyon walls and the tired team must push on to reach the take-out before dark, moving quickly through the next rapids. Then the river starts to mellow out and the end is near – warm clothes and a cold beer await the kayakers. As the take-out comes into sight all feelings of tiredness are forgotten, eyes sparkle and high fives sound out across the water. Another superb day's paddling in Tessin, life does not get any better.

**Grade**
3

**Experience**
Intermediate

**Getting there**
The Vorderrhein is in south-east Switzerland in the canton of Graubünden and both Reichenau and Ilanz are signposted from the motorway. Or fly to Zurich and it is just a two-hour train ride to Versam where you can hire a boat, paddle and gear from local outfitters

**In this location**
The Glenner joins the Vorderrhein in Ilanz and is the last natural flowing river in Graubuenden. For a more extreme adventure check out the Valserrhein or Medelserrhein

**On land**
The Vorderrhein and surrounding area is a tourist's paradise; hiking, biking, golf, spa, skiing or via ferrata, there is something for everybody there

# VORDERRHEIN RIVER, SWITZERLAND

## A wonderful range of rapids in a truly dramatic setting

Every country has a classic river, one every good paddler has kayaked, which paddlers young and old enjoy, where new paddlers share the eddy with pros. The Vorderrhein in Switzerland is such a river. Clear alpine water, jaw-dropping scenery and warm summer sun make a journey through the canyon of the Vorderrhein an enchanting day out for rafters and kayakers alike

The Vorderrhein is known as the Grand Canyon of Switzerland and is without a doubt one of the most visually stunning river trips in Europe. There are many things that make the Vorderrhein a special day's paddling. The first is the opportunity to load your canoe into the train in Reichenau and ride up alongside the river to the put-in at Ilanz; the train is quicker, environmentally friendlier and more relaxing than driving. A short walk from the train station brings you to the put-in just below the road bridge in Ilanz.

The Vorderrhein starts off gently, allowing you to warm up and get into the mood for an unforgettable day's paddling and take the opportunity to gaze around at the stunning surrounding mountains and scenery. Just over 12,000 years ago Europe's biggest landslide tumbled down from the Flimserstein on the left side of the river and completely blocked the path of the water; it took approximately 2,500 years of nature's power for the water to push back through the limestone debris and cut out the gorge we enjoy today, the Ruin'Alta (deep gorge).

As you progress down the Vorderrhein you will notice it becoming narrower and the river banks growing into rock walls. Get ready for action, you are entering the gorge! The pace picks up, the waves get bigger and the rapids longer and more technical, but don't panic, there are plenty of eddies to catch along the way. An old iron bridge signals the start of a short stretch of flowing water without rapids, a chance to relax and prepare for the most famous rapid on the river, Schwarzesloch (Black Hole). You hear the low rumbling of the rapids before you see them and then, Wow! A long technical rapid with big waves and rocks is a challenge for paddlers of all abilities, from a simple straight down top to bottom line, a complex parcours between rocks or surfing the many waves in the rapids, Schwarzesloch has something for every paddler.

The Vorderrhein continues on into the deepest and most beautiful part of the gorge below the village of Versam. The gorge is over 984-foot (300m) deep in places with numerous twists and turns, easier rapids and plenty of beaches to chill out on and eat a picnic lunch. The river slows and becomes wider, the rock walls sink back down to river banks and the gorge ends. The last stretch back to Reichenau is ideal to wind down and reflect upon your day's adventure. Basic rapids and a steady flow of water bring you back to your start point and the end of an ultimate canoe and kayak adventure.

kanuschule.ch

**Experience**
Novice

**Getting there**
A road runs along one shore of Wastwater, so it is easily accessed by car

**In this location**
The Lake District has an abundance of water but unfortunately not all of the lakes have access. Derwent Water, Windermere and Ullswater, however, all have good access

**On land**
The Lake District is a haven for those who love the outdoors. If you're feeling fit why not combine a paddle on England's deepest lake with a walk to the top of its highest mountain?

# WASTWATER, LAKE DISTRICT, ENGLAND

## Drifting on England's deepest lake

Wastwater, England's deepest lake, is situated in the wild and remote valley of Wasdale in the south-western fells of England's Lake District. So stunning is the vista, on a sunny and windless day, as you look down the lake towards Dale Head, that it was awarded the prestigious title of 'Britain's Favourite View'.

With a resumé like that you'd think that the surface of Wastwater would be crammed with boats, but not so. Even though there is a limit of only 12 canoes allowed on the lake at one time, this is a moot point as its remote location means that, even in the holiday season, it very rarely gets more than a few canoes on it at one time and the likelihood is that you will have the entire lake to yourself.

The secluded location is one of the features that is most appealing to paddlers. The lake is isolated, unspoilt, tranquil, and a truly beautiful area of the Lake District National Park. At nearly three miles (5km) long, almost half-a-mile (0.8km) wide and, with a depth of 258 feet (79m), Wastwater, at its deepest is below sea level. Add to this the fact that it is overlooked by England's highest mountain, Scafell Pike at 3,210 feet (978m), and it becomes an area of dramatic extremes that cries out to be explored by canoe.

As soon as you set off you'll feel the power of the location, the mountains that surround you and the dramatic Lakeland. The mirror-flat water is crystal clear, but suddenly the lake bed appears to drop away rapidly. The water beneath you becomes inky black and you can only imagine how far above the very bottom you are.

The peace and solitude of Wastwater, coupled with the characteristic brooding feel of the valley, is a huge contrast to some of the more popular of the Lake District's lakes. Wordsworth described Wastwater as 'long, stern and desolate' and as you glide across its surface you'll understand how this landscape has inspired painters, poets, climbers, and now canoeists, over the centuries.

Access to the lake is easy and there are several places where you can park a vehicle and easily carry your canoe down to the water's edge. How you choose to explore the lake is up to you, but a circumnavigation will let you take in every aspect. There are a few places along the shoreline that lend themselves to a stop for a well-earned cup of coffee, but the gravel beaches next to Low Woods at the south-western end of the lake make an ideal lunch spot as you can tuck in to your refreshments while gazing down the length of Wastwater at 'That View'.

**Experience**
Novice - Expert

**Getting there**
Devizes is situated in the county of Wiltshire near the main M4 motorway. The nearest airports are Heathrow and Bristol for visiting international crews

**In this location**
In the months leading up to the DW there are a series of shorter races known as the Watersides. These are usually used as training for the main Devizes to Westminster Race

**On land**
The race is going to be your main focus but the bright lights of London are home to a wealth of restaurants, bars, museums and galleries if you have any energy left to take advantage of them!

# DEVIZES TO WESTMINSTER, ENGLAND

## 125-mile canoe race – an ultimate test of endurance

Often referred to as the racing kayaker's Everest, the origins of the Devizes to Westminster Canoe Race, or DW as it is commonly known, begin way back in 1920 when regulars in the Greyhound pub in the sleepy village of Pewsey, spurred on by a national bus and rail strike, were debating the possibilities of other methods of transport. A wager was made. Was it possible to travel the 70 miles (112km) from Pewsey, along the River Avon to the sea, in under three days? This gauntlet was taken up and a sculling skiff, loaded with four determined gentleman, won the bet!

Many years later, after another lively debate in the Greyhound, the 'Avon to the sea' challenge was resurrected and a prize offered, which attracted the interest of a local scoutmaster from nearby Devizes. He wanted his scouts to take part in their canoes, but the prize was specifically for skiffs and Pewesy residents. The scoutmaster needed a different challenge. As luck would have it a former Avon racer had hatched a plan to try to reach London using the Kennet and Avon Canal and the River Thames in less than 100 hours. His plan fell through but the Devizes scouts gamely picked up the challenge. Easter 1948, Brian Smith, Brian Walters, Laurie Jones and Peter Brown launched onto the canal at Devizes. 89 hours and 50 minutes later they arrived at Westminster to the cheers of the waiting crowds. The DW had been born!

In its early years the race was dominated by the armed services, as their physical fitness, discipline and organisational skills fitted well with the race's challenge. A reliable support team is essential.

The modern DW race can be attempted in any kind of kayak or canoe, but be warned; over the course of the race there are many, many portages so a racing kayak is still the preferred weapon of choice. Single kayaks and juniors now have to stop over night, but the hardy souls of the two-man K2 class are permitted to paddle throughout the night! It's mentally and physically demanding. As you power along the 54 miles (87km) of the Kennet & Avon Canal, with the current record of just over 15 hours on your mind, Westminster will seem a long, long way away.

At the town of Reading you finally join the River Thames and the race is on to reach Teddington Lock. After this the Thames is tidal, so it's imperative to time your run to allow you to catch the outgoing or slack tide. Get it wrong and it can spell the end of your race. From there it's a tough slog on the wide rolling waters of Ol' Father Thames until you finally pass the impressive Houses of Parliament and the iconic tower of Big Ben. Pass under Westminster Bridge and it's all over. You've done it; you've scaled the heights of the canoe racer's Everest. Your body will ache for weeks but the sense of achievement is overwhelming. It's addictive too. Once the DW gets in your blood you'll be coming back for more, year after year after year!

**Experience**
Novice
Paddling a stable packraft on flatwater is easy and intuitive. Always wear a buoyancy aid

**Getting there**
Besides buses, Paddington Station backs onto the Canal, and the Docklands Light Railway (DLR) passes close to Limehouse Basin. You need a permit from the Canal Rivers Trust or British Canoeing

**In this location**
Another easy canal paddle goes from Limehouse up to the Olympic Park and beyond. And there's always the Thames – no permit needed but with big tides and other craft, you need to be alert. Visit the Port of London Authority website. Early mornings downstream on an ebbing tide is best, before the tourist boats get going

**On land**
It's London, knock yourself out!

# REGENT'S CANAL, LONDON, ENGLAND

## An urban packraft safari

A packraft is a portable raft that weighs from 4.5 pounds (2kg) and can be unrolled and inflated anywhere. For most users packrafts open up a new way of accessing remote wilderness areas (see p118). But a packraft is also a great way of exploring urban waterways. Excellent transport links make cities ideal venues for easily deployed packrafts.

Britain's urban canals have long been reborn as quaint, idiosyncratic backwaters for boat dwellers, joggers and cycle commuters. Former industrial wastelands have been transformed into glitzy apartment blocks or waterside business parks complete with mouth-watering eateries and amusing sculptures. The old cliche of filthy neglected ditches where joy-riders dumped stolen scooters and drunks hurled traffic cones is largely outdated, at least in central London.

For millennia waterways were the original transport superhighways and man-made canals connected river navigations to inland manufacturing hubs and busy seaports. Barges inexpensively moved heavy, bulky or fragile commodities unsuited to Britain's derelict Roman-era roads. The 200-year-old Regent's Canal is inner London's best example, arcing nearly nine miles (14.5km) from Paddington eastwards to Limehouse on the Thames. It was built to link the Grand Union Canal from the industrial heartlands around Birmingham, with the Thames' tidal reach near the new West India Docks, then the commercial hub of Britain's maritime empire.

Start in the urban canyon of glass and steel that is Paddington Basin, close to the station. Passing still cobbled wharves, you soon reach the willowy moorings of Little Venice, where horse-drawn barges once exchanged cargoes for the journey back north. Nearby is the arrow-straight, 820-foot (250m) Maida Hill tunnel, officially closed to solo unpowered craft. It leads to Regent's Park's neoclassical mansions and the chattering apes of London Zoo, before turning for Camden Lock Market where Jimi Hendrix bought his first Rosetti Airstream.

At Camden it's easier to portage and tow a trio of locks (there are 13 in total) before arriving at redeveloped King's Cross, home to Google UK, the Word on the Water floating bookshop and giant Victorian gas storage tanks repurposed into luxury flats. The London Canal Museum is nearby in Battlebridge Basin.

East of here, air down and portage around the half-mile (880m) long Islington Tunnel before resuming your newt's- eye traverse, flitting between bohemian, suburban, light industrial, and even rural parkland, as well as historical relics dating back to the canal's commercial heyday.

In high summer thick duckweed (Spirodela polyrhiza) can carpet the surface, and you might spot a feral turtle perching on a half-sunk canoe. Finally you arrive at Limehouse Basin alongside the Thames, not far from the business and financial district of Canary Wharf, the modern commercial hub of the capital.

With the right tide, you could close the loop and paddle back upriver towards Westminster, or more easily set off downstream for Greenwich. But that's another urban packrafting adventure.

**Experience**
Intermediate – Expert

**Getting there**
From Norwich, take the A47 to Great Yarmouth, or head north towards Wroxham, Stalham and Petter Heigham. Wroxham is the end of the line for the Bure Valley Railway

**In this location**
Located just south-east of Norwich, Whitlingham Country Park is a wooded water park built on an old quarry site. It offers a wealth of water activities. Craft hire and water permits can be purchased

**On land**
There is plenty to do off the water. Visit Wroxham Barns for shopping, crafts and a junior farm. In Hoveton visit the Hoveton Hall gardens and church of St Peter, built in 1624. Near Ranworth, take in the ruins of St Benet's Abbey, whose writings date back to the 13th century, and visit the Museum of the Broads in Stalham

# NORFOLK BROADS, ENGLAND

## UK utopia – a gentle delight for paddlers

Is there a more concentrated and user-friendly network of canoeing and kayaking trails than the UK's Norfolk Broads? Billed as the country's largest wetlands region, the area features a maze of inter-connected rivers, marshes and lakes, letting you paddle inn-to-inn, base camp out of a B&B, or camp along the way.

The arteries are a result of countless years of peat digging during the Middle Ages for fuel. Over time, the pits and trenches filled in with water, which have now formed a network of 125 miles (201km) of forested and open waterways perfect for paddlers of all levels. No matter which route you take, you'll paddle among butterflies, dragonflies, birds, otters and more.

The main river in the system is the Bure, which runs from above Aylsham to the town of Great Yarmouth. With paddling above Buxton littered with portages and access issues, the easiest access at Buxton is via TheCanoeMan centre, which offers everything from rentals to parking. From here to Coltishall the river winds through open grasslands and forests. Below, as the river continues on to Wroxham (the capital of the Broads), you have to dodge motorboaters, especially below Wroxham, where

the river widens and the main Broads run begins.

At Honing, the Ant River offers another good option. Widening as it snakes its way downstream, the river changes from a narrow, reed-lined stream into the North Walsham Canal, and then widens more past the A149 bridge down to Barton Broad, one of the best regions for spotting wildlife. Access and parking can be found at Barton Turf, and further down at the Irstead church and Ludham bridge before the river joins the Bure at St Benet's Abbey.

One of the prettiest rivers to paddle in the Norfolk region is the Wensum, which winds from Fakenham to Attlebridge. While its upper reaches are often clogged with trees, its lower stretches offer plenty of prime, forested paddling (beware the portage in the middle) and angling; it's the only Norfolk area river to harbour barbel and trout. After winding through open farmland, it runs through Norwich before joining the Yare.

One of the more difficult rivers in the region, the Yare, is best paddled from below the Earlham church down to Cringleford and, eventually, Trowse, where it starts to widen before its confluence with the Wensum.

Another popular paddle in the Norfolk Broads region is the Waveney, which meanders along the Norfolk / Suffolk border. A favourite starting point is Scole, below which you'll find forested hillsides, gently flowing currents and plenty of wildlife. Expect motorboat traffic below Geldeston Lock, where it widens and becomes more tidal.

**Experience**
Intermediate

**Getting there**
Lee Bay is just outside the town of Ilfracombe on the North Devon coast of England and easily accessed by road

**In this location**
There are innumerable great sea kayaking trips around this part of England's coast. Standout trips are from Ilfracombe to Lynton, and from Hartland Quay, along the Hartland Heritage Coast, to the town of Westward Ho!

**On land**
On Lundy there's plenty to see and do, it's home to Old Light, built on the highest base for a lighthouse in Britain, so pack a pair of walking shoes. A guided walk, led by one of the island's wardens is a great way to learn more about this fascinating place. Or you can simply wile away some time enjoying the 'experience' in the Marisco Tavern and swapping tall tales of the sea with other visitors

# LUNDY ISLAND, ENGLAND

## This sea kayak crossing is a must-do adventure

The Island of Lundy is three miles long (5km) and 465 feet (142m) high and sits haughtily, an imposing chunk of granite surrounded by tidal races, off the coast of North Devon, where the Atlantic Ocean meets the Bristol Channel. On a fine day its shimmering appearance from the mainland calls out to sea kayakers, like some great granite siren, to brave the 12-mile (19km) open crossing.

The island and its surrounding waters are abounding with wildlife, and the whole area has been designated as a Site of Special Scientific Interest. It was also England's first statutory Marine Nature Reserve.

Although the tides are strong and careful planning and preparation are necessary to make a safe, successful crossing you don't need to be a heroic sea dog, born with a paddle in one hand and a sextant in the other to make the crossing to Lundy.

There are two usual departure points for a trip across by sea kayak, one is Hartland Quay and the other, more commonly used, is Lee Bay. Although longer in distance, the Lee Bay crossing is easier and

understandably more popular. A good weather window will be needed so it pays to keep a close eye on the forecast for a period of calm, stable weather.

The journey can take between three and five hours and starts by taking you out from Lee Bay and round Bull Point and its passing tidal race. This can present challenging waves in certain conditions. Once past this the crossing should be uneventful, providing you got that weather forecast right, and you will plug away towards your goal, paddling on a compass bearing until Lundy finally comes into view. Although this section of the journey is fairly straightforward, keep your eyes peeled as it is not uncommon to encounter porpoise, dolphins and even basking shark.

Your aim is to reach the Landing Beach, which lies below the South Light Lighthouse on the south-east of the island. As you approach conditions can again be testing, with the tide attempting to sweep you southwards. Once safely on land, you can head straight to the campsite, or visit the fantastic Marisco Tavern for a well-deserved pint of foaming locally brewed ale.

To really get the most out of a visit to Lundy it is best done over three days: the paddle out on the first, then a circumnavigation of the island and its sea caves, arches and cliffs teeming with birdlife. The final day is then spent reversing your original journey until you once again paddle past Bull Point and arrive back at Lee Bay, tired but happy at completing one of the best sea kayak trips that England has to offer.

**Grade**
4+

**Experience**
Intermediate – Expert

**Getting there**
Dartmeet sits in the Dartmoor National Park and is easily accessed by road. The nearest towns are Ashburton or Princetown. The closest international airports are in Exeter and Bristol

**In this location**
If you want a change of pace, the middle section of the Dart, known as The Loop, provides some grade 3 whitewater. If you want to keep up the intensity, the nearby River Plym, River Erme and Upper Walkham will keep the adrenaline pumping. The north and south Devonshire coastlines are a couple of hours away, so kayak surfing and sea kayaking are another option

**On land**
Dartmoor is perfect for all sorts of outdoor action. Horse riding, mountain biking and walking are popular and the moor's rocky granite attracts those who like to climb

# RIVER DART, ENGLAND

## Devonshire cream – England's finest whitewater run

The Upper Dart flows from high amongst the rocky tors of the historic and atmospheric Dartmoor, in the English county of Devon. The Dart is formed when the East and West Dart come together at the aptly named Dartmeet. At its end it flows slowly out to the sea at Dartmouth but in its upper reaches, as it crashes over steep granite bedrock, it is arguably the best stretch of whitewater, at its grade, in England.

At all levels the run is a stiff challenge and is rightly considered a test piece; and when the rains come, as the peat coloured water pours from the moor, and the level rises, it becomes very serious indeed. It's to be treated with respect as its nature is continuous and its setting in a deep gorge nestled high on the moor makes it a very difficult river to walk out of if things go wrong. It has seen its fair share of serious incidents, so treat it like a mini-expedition and maybe run it at a low to middle level as your first go. In higher water the lines stay fairly similar but it becomes even more continuous and there are some big holes hiding to gobble up the unwary or the unprepared. In very high water it's fair to say that the Upper becomes a religious experience. Even hardened whitewater warriors fresh off the boat after a season of running waterfalls in Norway have come drifting out at the end with faces as white as snow and a far away look in their eyes.

The great thing about the Upper is that it always delivers at whatever level. In low levels the first few rapids and the paddle out can become scrappy and a bit of a drag but the meat of the run will still have you grinning. As the level increases, various moves come in to play and the adrenaline levels rise along with the water. Because it's granite, the Dart can rise and fall quickly, so pay attention to the forecast and prevailing conditions. If it is, or has been, raining it's possible to get on at a medium level and then find yourself roaring along on a high flow by the time you're halfway down.

The river weaves its way down, a ribbon of unbroken white, through boulder gardens and over ledges. Rapid after rapid comes at you thick and fast with a flurry of excellent ledge-style drops. There are a few good 'rock' moves in there too if you want to add even more spice to your run.

If you're finding your flow you'll be paddling hard and grinning from ear to ear. Highlights include the descriptively named Mad Mile, Euthanasia Falls and Sharah's Pool, also often called Surprise, Surprise!

The quality of its whitewater and the wild and beautiful setting combine to make the Upper Dart an absolute classic and you'll be grinning like the kayaking cat that got the Devonshire Cream at the take-out.

**Experience**
Intermediate – Expert

**Getting there**
Most people either fly or take the ferry (note: you can't bring a vehicle). If ferrying, reserve a spot for yourself and your kayak (including return) well in advance

**In this location**
You can also take a multi-day tour along Britain's south-west coast exploring sea caves, coves, wrecks and beaches. If you're brave and skilled enough, you can paddle the 28 miles (45km) from Land's End to the Isles, depending on the tides and weather. But beware the currents and shipping lanes; make sure you have the proper equipment, safety plans and skills

**On land**
St Mary's has 30 miles (48km) of coastal paths and nature trails. A popular walk leads around the Garrison, offering stunning views of the other islands

# ISLES OF SCILLY, UK

## Stunning waters and a uniquely warm climate

Multi-day sea kayak trips don't always have to involve trying to find the perfect campsite. In the Isles of Scilly – a network of more than 100 islands and rocks, most boasting white sand beaches, exotic plants and wildlife, just 28 miles (45km) west of England's westernmost point – you can paddle for days on end, returning each evening to the comfort of a B&B.

Of course, you can camp if you want to as well; but it has to be at a designated site. The whole area has been designated a Special Area of Conservation, meaning no 'wild' camping is allowed. While the sites are somewhat developed, that's a small price to pay for access to prime paddling.

There are well-equipped campsites on four of the inhabited islands – St Mary's, St Agnes, St Martin's and Bryher, with St Agnes and St Martin's islands offering campsites next to the beach. Each comes with a range of amenities, including showers, toilets, hot and cold water, washing machines, tumble dryers and more. Most also either have a small grocery store or are close to one (as well as pubs at which you can tell your day's paddling tale). Only five of the islands are inhabited, with most inhabitants living in the village of Hugh Town on St Mary's, the group's largest island.

Each island has its own character and story to tell, many reflected in their names such as Kettle Bottom, Hunter's Lump and Great Cheese Rock. Tean and St Helen's have the remains of early Christian chapels, with the latter also supposedly harbouring the burial site of St Elidius, a British bishop and son of an English King. Paddle by aptly named Round Island and you can tour an historic lighthouse, and set your rudder for Samson and you can get out to see prehistoric monuments. You can also revel in everything from seals to shipwrecks, with the Western Rocks containing a memorial to the lost ships and seamen before Bishop Rock was crowned with the UK's most south-westerly lighthouse.

In short, a typical paddle takes you past everything from Civil War castles and prehistoric sites to nooks, crannies and slots formed between rocky outcroppings. It's a paddling playground, suitable for sea kayakers of all abilities. Conditions range from clear, tranquil waters protected by bays to easy crossings, crashing surf and rolling swell percolating its way across the Atlantic.

Keep your eyes peeled for wildlife, as the area's rich nutrients lure a wealth of marine animals to the region (many parties head to the Isles in May when marine life is most prevalent). On a typical day you can expect to see a variety of sea birds, as well as dolphins, basking sharks and seals.

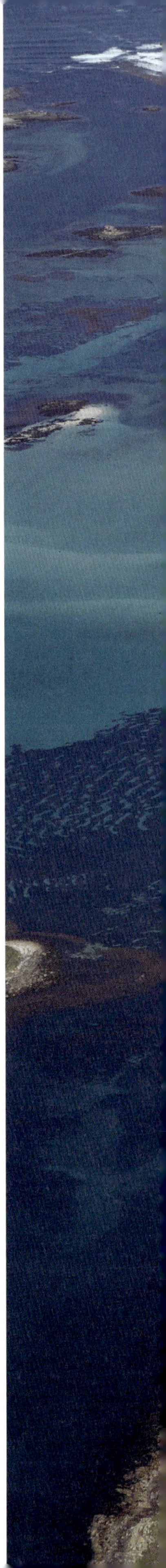

**Grade**
1-2

**Experience**
Novice – Intermediate

**Getting there**
Peebles is the most popular put-in for the River Tweed. It is possible to hire canoes and equipment from local outfitters. Most outfitters also arrange a shuttle drop for you in Peebles and collect you a few days later in Coldstream or Berwick-upon-Tweed

**In this location**
The east coast of Scotland is an incredible place for sea kayaking. Scotland is the home to countless incredible whitewater rivers for adrenaline-hungry paddlers of all abilities

**On land**
The River Tweed is a world famous salmon fishing river. There are many castles and watch-towers to explore. There is a multitude of mountain biking routes in Kielder Forest and a myriad of opportunities for hiking and walking

# RIVER TWEED, SCOTLAND

## An increadibly beautiful river

Not only is it a highlight for canoeists and kayakers, the River Tweed is also regarded as one of the best salmon fisheries in the world.

A multi-day journey in an open canoe or kayak along the River Tweed on the Scottish-English border is one of the best beginner trips in the UK; superb scenery, fun rapids that can be easily portaged for those not confident enough to tackle them and an accommodation choice of hotels or wild camping, this river has everything.

The Tweed has a very relaxed character, and you can easily drift off into another world as the flow gently carries you and your canoe along, but try to keep alert as there are many small rapids and ripples to entertain the more adventurous paddler. The first rapid is at Yair Cauld. The Fairilee, an enjoyable class 2 rapid, can be easily portaged for beginners who don't fancy testing themselves to the limit.

The next challenging rapid is not far away, Melrose Cauld. It is tricky to inspect and has a reputation as a rocky rapid that has damaged canoes: the consequences of damaging your boat on a multi-day trip are much greater than when on a local journey. There are many beautiful places where one can set up camp along the banks of the River Tweed. Wild camping is one of the most exciting parts of a multi-day adventure; selecting, packing and transporting everything you need to survive comfortably in the outdoors. The feeling of total self sufficiency is awesome. A tent or tarp, a warm sleeping bag and air bed, a hot cup of tea and a tasty evening meal cooked on an open fire followed by a wee dram of the Highland's finest whisky, there isn't a five star hotel in the world that can create such an atmosphere, just you, your chosen travelling buddies and the wilderness.

The most tricky rapids on the Tweed are found above Kelso – the Makerstoun rapids are a series of four drops that will raise the heartbeat for all. Depending on the water levels canoeists may choose to portage, take the easier line on river right or the more adventurous line in the middle, there are even a few eddies to catch on the way down for show-offs!

The River Tweed can be enjoyed all year round: in summer the flow is normally at its least, the weather is perfect for living outdoors, but the rapids can be quite technical, and in autumn and winter the crisp clean air conjures up a very special atmosphere, for experienced campers the chilly temperatures are no problem.

**Experience**
Intermediate – Expert

**Getting there**
Most visitors arrive in the main town and capital city of Stornoway on the ferry from Ullapool – a crossing of about three hours. For flights, your best bet is to fly into Inverness and transfer from there

**In this location**
Why restrict yourself to the Outer Hebrides? The Inner Hebrides, including the Sound of Arisaig, offer a wealth of paddling options as well, with white, sandy beaches and beautiful backdrops, including the Isles of Rum, Eigg and Muck

**On land**
The Outer Hebrides are one of Scotland's best kept secrets for walking and hiking. Plan a day or two to let your legs do the work and get up high so you can take in the commanding views

# OUTER HEBRIDES, SCOTLAND

## The jewel in Scotland's crown

The Outer Hebrides boast some of the best sea kayaking in Scotland, if not the world, with turquoise waters, great wildlife and stunning scenery.

Located off the mainland's north-west coast, the Outer Hebrides are separated from the Scottish mainland and the Inner Hebrides by the waters of the Minch Strait, Little Minch and the Sea of Hebrides. In all, the island group contains 15 inhabited islands and more than 50 uninhabited islands bigger than 100 acres (0.4km$^2$), comprising a veritable slalom course for sea kayakers.

The group's major islands include Lewis, Harris, North and South Uist, Barra and Bennecula. Connected by a land bridge, together Lewis and Harris comprise the largest island in Scotland and the third largest in the British Isles after Great Britain and Ireland.

Lewis itself is the largest and most populated of the group, with the capital, Stornoway, home to nearly 10,000 people and where most paddlers begin their trip. Its landscape of peat-covered bedrock gives way to mountains on its west side, harbouring coastal beaches for camping and kayaking. There

you'll also find such historic relics as the Standing Stones of Callanish, dating from before Stonehenge, and brochs, massive round towers used as forts, which spread to the Hebrides around 200 BC. One of the best – the Iron Age round house known as Dun Carloway – is also located on the west coast of Lewis.

Immediately south of Lewis is sparsely populated and mountainous Harris, whose peaks tower 2,560 feet (780m) high and offer views of the distant island group of St Kilda. Its west coast also has great beaches for landing and camping, including the largest sand dunes in Europe. And lest you think the blue sea and sky (if it's not grey and raining) is the only colour you'll see, many of the beaches are also lined with the vibrant blooms of the flowers of the machair.

While you can break camp daily, many paddlers also opt to base camp at more established sites, many of which offer such facilities as showers and toilets, and explore the area with lighter, empty boats by either driving to different launch points or going solely by paddle power.

Other popular paddling spots include the islands of Loch Roag and the west coastline of Great Bernera.

Regardless of where you head and how you choose to spend your evenings, a week passes as easily as the kayaking miles in the area, especially with daylight lasting almost until midnight in the summer. Just pay attention to the weather and sea conditions and keep your itinerary flexible. Besides, if it's inclement weather, you can always break out the bagpipes.

WHITEWATER

**Grade**
4-4+

**Experience**
Expert

**Getting there**
The Etive is situated in the Western Highlands and is easily accessed by car from Glen Coe and Fort William. Glasgow Airport is about two hours away

**In this location**
Too much to mention. This area of Scotland is blessed with an abundance of fantastic whitewater rivers, but within a short drive of Glen Etive are the Coe and the Leven

**On land**
As well as the brilliant whitewater rivers of the region it's a Mecca for hill walkers, climbers and mountain bikers. In the wintertime the nearby Glen Coe Ski resort can provide fun for snow-sports enthusiasts

# GLEN ETIVE, SCOTLAND

## The granite slides of Scotland's triple crown

The River Etive is rightfully considered a classic Scottish run. With its rapids, smooth boulder gardens, tight constrictions and exhilarating slides it can provide a stiff challenge. Slide into its chilly waters and the action begins immediately as you line yourself up for the first rapid. From then on in you are contained between the river's high granite walls as you negotiate your way down its various challenges.

Dynamic paddling will be rewarded and there's always a moment of calm at the end of each drop. If you can take your eyes off the crashing whitewater you'll be greeted with a breathtaking view of the cascading river and steep-sided granite walls.

From start to finish kayakers will enjoy a roller-coaster ride until they reach the final challenge, the tricky dog-leg rapid that leads into the diminutive pool above the lip of Right Angle Falls. The fall drops cleanly into a natural amphitheatre, where, as you slide out of the pool and over the sloping lip, you will enjoy a fleeting feeling of freefall, before you crash deep into the foaming waters below. After you've taken a moment to calm down, it's a short but technical paddle down to the take-out opposite the Allt a'

Chaorainn, a tributary that flows into the Etive from the river's left bank.

For some this may be enough and the end of their day, but for those looking to complete the 'Triple Crown' it's time to paddle over to the opposite bank before shouldering your kayak for the short but steep hike to the top of the Allt a' Chaorainn.

This is a step up in gradient as the run supplies a series of nerve- wracking, but thrill-packed granite slab slides and drops with small flat pools in between. This is kayaking as a contact sport as you rattle down, ricocheting off rocks as you go.

A short drive will see you ready for the third and final challenge: the Allt Mheuran. It delivers a shot of almost pure excitement. Once unloaded you will need to hike your kayak down to the Etive and paddle it across to the far bank. You will need to shoulder your kayak and summon up your remaining strength for a tough climb up to the frothing chutes above.

The run starts with a 15-foot (5m) drop into a small pool, which leads directly to a twisting and turning granite gutter that becomes steeper as it goes and culminates in the kayaker flying down a 30-foot (9m) slide and launching over a 20-foot (6m) waterfall.

As you fly down that final slide, it really will feel like you are about to drop off the end of the world. You'll sit shaking in the bottom pool, looking back up from where you've just come – and you'll feel elated, invincible and alive.

**Experience**
Expert

**Getting there**
The Falls of Lora form pretty much under the historic Connel Bridge where the A828 road crosses the Firth before the village of Connel. You can either park outside the Oyster Inn, just over the bridge on the A85 or in the lay-by on the other side of the bridge and bushwhack through the trees

**In this location**
This area offers world-class paddling. For whitewater paddlers there are some absolute classics within driving distance, including the River Etive and its tributaries, and the Rivers Coe & Leven

**On land**
Oban is a Mecca for seafood and has fine restaurants and pubs. A visit to the Oban Distillery, one of Scotland's oldest sources of single malt Scotch whisky, is a great way to spend an hour or two. If it's adventure you're looking for then mountain biking, hill walking and diving are all on the agenda

# FALLS OF LORA, OBAN, SCOTLAND

## Sweet, glassy waves and a stunning highland setting

The Falls of Lora are situated six miles (9.7km) north-east of Oban, on the rugged West Coast of Scotland, and are formed when the level in the Firth of Lorn drops below the level of the water in Loch Etive as the tide ebbs.

When this happens the seawater in Loch Etive pours out through the narrows, which are spanned by the spectacular and historic Connel Bridge.

If the tides are right and the falls are running, they form a set of superb, glassy, standing waves. For many years the Falls of Lora were the preserve of local Scottish kayakers, but so good is the feature that, once the word got out, paddlers started to visit the falls from all over the world.

There are three main features of interest. First up is the Ultimate Wave, which forms out in the middle of the channel when the tide first begins to run. It's hollow and fast and really keeps you on your toes. As the tide builds the Ultimate Wave begins to fade until it becomes no more – but that is just the

appetiser, the main feast is just beginning.

A glassy, smooth wave known as the Forever Wave because once caught you can stay on it forever, will have now appeared. It's a truly sublime experience, carving from side to side across its face, with the inky black waters of Loch Etive rushing beneath the hull of your kayak. Look up as you surf and you'll gaze at a majestic Highland landscape unfolding out beyond the loch.

Behind the Forever Wave lies the main wave and this can change in character along with the tide. It begins as a steep, green wave, which builds in stature until it becomes a big green face with a large, and often violent, breaking pile. It's a wild ride, and the good and the brave like nothing more than slashing across the surging shoulder of the wave, pulling off freestyle moves and landing in the pit, then taking a few tumbles in the foaming chaos before regaining control and once more surfing out onto the shoulder.

Once you wash off the main wave you have to run the gauntlet of surging boiling water and vicious whirlpools to get back into the calm waters of the eddy that forms along the bank, so you can paddle back up and do it all again.

The secret of catching a classic day on the Falls of Lora is timing. Its tidal nature means it only really comes into peak condition at the big tides of the year and it can change according to local conditions. Kelp growing on the bottom of the loch can affect the wave, so some years it is bigger than others. Get it right though and arrive on a clear Highland day with a big spring tide running and you'll enjoy an experience that you'll never forget!

# LOCH ARD, SCOTLAND

## Explore the source of the Forth River

Loch Ard is a relatively small inland loch located in the Trossachs in the Central Belt of Scotland. The Trossachs boast some 17 lochs (including Loch Lomond and Scotland's only lake, the Lake of Menteith), which makes is the paddlers' dream in terms of exploring and adventuring. Some argue that Loch Ard is the source of the Forth River which ends up joining the North Sea by Edinburgh.

One tour option is the Narrows. Park at the east end of the loch lay-bys. The road winds about a bit and when it meets the main loch, the lay-bys are just on your right-hanxd side.

Launch over the wall where there's a wee sandy beach (it's a good spot for swimming too and watching the sunset). Head around to the left (east) and follow the shoreline until you find the gap in the rhododendron bushes. There is a cross on a rock just by the launch spot, keep an eye on your depth here.

This wee stream takes you down towards a couple of mini-lochs, lochans if you will, where the local houses have boat houses and swimming decks. Watch your fins here as it can be shallow depending on the time of year. There can also be a strong flow so please be mindful you do have to come back upstream to get back to your starting point.

It's absolutely stunning, especially on a wind-free day or in the autumn when the trees show off their colours. There is a barrier across the river proper so don't go past the second lochan.

The road by the loch can be flooded in periods of heavy rain, and if the wind dies away, be mindful of the midgies! They may descend as you are trying to pack up.

Another tour is at the west end to the secret loch and bothy. Park at the Kinlochard Village Hall, remembering to give a wee donation in the box, cross the road and through the gate, over the field and there's the remains of an old jetty you can launch from.

Over to your right there is a wee island with a bothy on it. If you continue past the island, there is another narrow opening with lily pads in the summer months hiding the entrance to a small, shallow lochan. This water here picks up the warmth so is a lovely sheltered spot for swimming or picnics. The forestry path round the loch passes close to the head of this lochan so if you have non-paddlers, they could walk up to meet you.

If you are looking for a little more distance, you can head down the loch following the southern shoreline and you will come across another tiny island called Eilean Gorm, the green isle. It's mostly rock to be honest and hosts the remains of Duke Murdoch's Castle. Nowadays it's used for jumping in and swimming.

If you keep your eyes peeled, you may also spot the cave where Rob Roy (a Scottish Robin Hood-type legend) is supposed to have hidden from Duke Murdoch during his smuggling runs.

**Experience**
Beginner – Expert
But please do check the forecast in advance and avoid offshore or stronger wind days which can make returning to your starting point a challenge

**Getting there**
Follow the Aberfoyle Road from Stirling or Glasgow. Once in Aberfoyle, at the Co-op head straight on instead of following the road round to the right. Park at the lay-bys at the east end of the loch, at Kinlochard Village Hall car park (donation) or at the lay-by at the Kinlochard end of the loch (but be mindful of the farmer who isn't a huge fan of paddlers trekking across his field)

**In this location**
More great paddling at Loch Chon nearby (further up the road) and Lake of Menteith (on the way to Loch Ard) – the only lake in Scotland

**On land**
Loch Ard Sculpture Trail, biking/hiking from the Forestry car park at the east end of the loch (brown signpost). Loch Katrine steamer, the *Sir Walter Scott* (can also walk/bike/paddle here). Go Ape at the Lodge, Forest Visitor Centre

**Experience**
Intermediate – Expert

**Getting there**
Anglesey has an airport on its south-west side at RAF Valley, less than two miles (3km) from the A55, with flights twice daily from Cardiff. To get to Anglesey from other destinations, use Manchester Airport, which offers easy access to North Wales from Europe, the U.S. and beyond. It has rail and road connections

**In this location**
After touring Holy Island, head back over to explore Anglesey Island and the Llŷn Peninsula. You can spend days exploring its nooks, crannies and sea caves

**On land**
Ever wanted to try climbing? There's no better place than nearby Eryi (Snowdonia National Park). Tell the day's tale of climbing or kayaking over a pint at Paddler's Return Bar in Porth Dafarch, whose walls display years of British sea kayaking history in the form of boats, newspaper clippings and other memorabilia

# ANGLESEY & HOLY ISLAND, WALES

## Getting wet in Wales

Offering calm flats for touring and waves for surfing, Anglesey offers a whale of a time for sea kayakers, from beginners to seasoned pros. The region has produced some of the UK's best paddlers (does Nigel Dennis ring a bell?), and has been hosting the annual Anglesey Sea Kayak Symposium for 40 years, one of the world's most prestigious sea kayaking events.

Of course, the main reason people come is the paddling. And it doesn't get any better than the west side of Anglesey, where Holy Island serves up everything from sheltered flat water to tidal waves for surfing. If that's not enough, Holy Island can also test your rock-dodging skills at Rhoscolyn, and even your strength and stamina at the tide races of The Stacks. Experts say that if you can paddle here, you can paddle anywhere.

You can paddle all the way around Holy Island or tackle different sections. One of the best routes is to start at Rhoscolyn or Trearddur Bay and tour south along a rocky coastline filled with arches (look for White Arch near Rhoscolyn Head) and caves. Just be aware of the tides; a passage or arch navigable at high water can leave you high and dry at low tide. Also prepare for varying currents, especially near Rhoscolyn Head where the tide funnels between outcroppings. And know that all your miscues will likely have an audience of seals. After passing the Valley RAF base and Silver Bay you'll head up Cymyran Strait to Four Mile Bridge.

A harder option is the Stacks – North, South and Penrhyn Mawr – that contain some of the fastest tides in the region. Most paddlers launch at the beach at Porth Dafarch and paddle to Penrhyn Mawr at high tide. To stretch your legs, climb the cliff at Porth Ruffydd for a scenic view. At South Stack you can also tour below a lighthouse and take in some of the area's best geology, including giant folds emulating the waves themselves. Near North Stack, keep your eyes peeled on the cliffs above Gogarth Bay for climbers and poke your bow into such sea caves as Parliament, a few of which allow you to paddle through.

The price of this paddling playground is dealing with the changing tides (one tidal race reaches 6 knots [11kph] and runs up to seven miles [11km] offshore). Check your charts and ask locals for advice before heading out (pick up a copy of *Cruising Anglesey and Adjoining Waters* by Ralph Morris). There are also a number of paddling shops and outfitters, including UK Sea Kayaking, Rockpool Kayaks and Rock and Sea, which can also offer suggestions.

**Grade**
4

**Experience**
Intermediate

**Getting there**
Ramsay Sound is close to St David's. A trip to the Bitches is not to be taken lightly and planning is needed before you go. Your timing needs to be spot on to make the paddle out successful. Carry a strobe light with you on your PFD and log in and out with the Coastguard

**In this location**
The Pembrokeshire coast is an ideal location for sea kayaking and the nearby surf beaches of Whitesands and Newgale are great for kayak surfing

**On land**
The whole area is part of the Pembrokeshire National Park and there are a myriad of walks and cycle rides on offer. Local specialities are surfing and coasteering, which involves donning a wetsuit, helmet and PFD and exploring the rugged coastline

# BITCHES TIDAL RACE, WALES

## An awe-inspiring place to paddle a kayak

The Bitches are a line of jagged rocks that protrude out from Ramsay Island into Ramsay Sound, and the tidal race which they produce is a soul surfer's paradise. Boats avoid them at all costs, but when a big tide runs. the dark water thunders through creating a series of features that will thrill and terrify in equal measure. No wonder the Bitches draw in whitewater kayakers from all over the world.

The features change slightly on different tides, but the two mainstays are the Hole of Soul and the glass-like top wave. The Bitches has a rightful claim to being the birthplace of UK whitewater freestyle paddling and indeed in 1991 the Bitches was host to the very first World Freestyle Kayaking Championships or, as it was called back then, 'whitewater rodeo'. Paddlers came from Europe and even as far as the United States to compete in this magical arena, and for many years afterwards the Bitches was home to big competitions and even bigger parties.

As good as the waves are, the thing that makes the Bitches such an epic adventure is the splendour

and exposed nature of their location. The Pembrokeshire coast is a place of rugged beauty and the Bitches sit just off Ramsay Island, a protected nature reserve, so it's not uncommon to see seals and even porpoise on the paddle out. To get there kayakers launch at slack water from below the lifeboat station at St Justinian on the mainland and then paddle up and then across the sound. It's a long way in a whitewater playboat! Then you sit and wait for the tide to run.

At first it just begins to build small waves and overfalls, but in no time at all it's honking through, the whole sound seems to be roaring like a freight train and the wave and hole are there in all their glorious, foaming, crashing form. You paddle hard out from behind the Big Bitch rock, lungs screaming and arms aching as you work to make the ferry glide across on to the top wave.

Then suddenly it all goes quiet as you feel your boat start to glide down the face of the wave. You've made it. Sea birds wheel overhead and you are aware of the shouts of your friends as they cheer you on. You carve the wave from side to side in graceful arcs listening to the hiss of the spray flying up from your bow. You are in the now, you are alive; you are Bitching!

Eventually the wave surges and the spell is broken as you wash off into the boiling chaos behind, fighting folding waves and whirlpools before you regain the relative calm of the eddy before once more taking your turn at the chance of another slice of soul-surfing bliss.

**Grade**
5

**Experience**
Expert

**Getting there**
Situated in Eryri (Snowdonia National Park), north Wales, you'll need a car to get you to the put-in at the car park near Penmachno Bridge and another parked near the take-out at Lyln-yr-Afanc (the Beaver Pool)

**In this location**
This region is a veritable Mecca for whitewater kayakers in the UK and it boasts more than its fair share of classics. Standouts include the Ogwen, the Llugwy and the Lledr. If you fancy a change of pace then the coast is not far away with some sea kayaking

**On land**
Eryri (Snowdonia) is bristling with activities. There is mountain biking, rock climbing, hill walking and mountaineering options. A visit to the area isn't complete without an ascent of Yr Wyddfa (Mount Snowdon), the second highest peak in the UK

# FAIRY GLEN, SNOWDONIA / ERYRI, WALES

## Experience your own Welsh whitewater fairytale

The Fairy Glen ... the name may invoke visions of tiny winged folk frolicking on the banks of a sun-dappled stream, but the reality is a difficult and demanding section of the River Conwy, roaring in a dark, imposing gorge in the shadow of the mountains of Eryri (Snowdonia) in north Wales. But don't be mistaken, the Fairy Glen is still a place of magic and mystery for the whitewater kayakers who come to take on the challenges of its dramatic drops.

The Conwy offer a variety of different sections of whitewater sport, but the Fairy Glen is its undisputed jewel in its moss-covered crown.

The Glen is situated not far from Betws-y-Coed, the principal village of Eryri (Snowdonia National Park). It's an area steeped in myth, legend and history and the area has been populated since Neolithic times.

As you make your way down the slippery muddy trail, below the Penmachno Bridge car park, which leads to the put-in, worn into the ground by generations of kayakers' river shoes, you'd be forgiven if you felt the flutter of a few fairies in your stomach. The sense of anticipation is palpable. As raindrops drip from the over-hanging trees you'll catch a glimpse of the Conwy running thick, foaming and brown through the undergrowth. The river's colour signals that the Glen is running at a good level and the first squirts of adrenaline will flow into your system ready for the thrills to come.

You'll need to control it though and force your brain to focus as there's no warm up and the action starts right from the very first eddy. You need to strap on your game face, snap on your deck and go. You'll need all your wits, attention and skills because the Fairy Glen demands your respect. Get into the groove and hit the sublime lines and challenging moves and you'll feel its magic fill your muscles with energy and your heart with joy. Be warned though, the Glen has a dark side too and it punishes the unprepared, the unlucky and the disrespectful with harsh, unforgiving and even fatal consequences. It deserves its big reputation.

The main crux of the run is the intimidating Fairy Falls and it'll seem that the river has grown large black, rocky teeth as you line yourself up above the lip. Other rapid names are no less atmospheric, The Doors of Perception, The Gates of Delirium and Pipeline.

The Fairy Glen section of the Conwy is without doubt one of the outstanding stretches of quality whitewater in the UK, and it's rightly considered a challenging test piece by local and visiting kayakers alike! In recent years it has become popular to push things a little further with paddlers seeing how fast they can go, or how many times it can be run in a day.

No surprise really, because once the Fairy Glen has cast its spell on you you'll be drawn back to run its dark and magical waters again and again and again.

**Experience**
Intermediate

**Getting there**
Travel by road to Trefor, Gwynedd; free car parking can be found adjacent to the harbour. Public transport available to the village centre from either Pwllheli (national rail connection) or Caernarfon

**In this location**
The Llŷn Peninsula is an Area of Outstanding Natural Beauty (ANOB) and boasts almost 100 miles (160km) of coastline, made up of sweeping bays and cliffs, perfect for paddlers of all types

**On land**
The Wales Coast Path offers cliff top walks, beach strolls and wildlife spotting in abundance. Nant Gwrtheyrn is home to a Welsh language centre. The three peaks of Yr Eifl (Garn For, Garn Ganol and Tre'r Ceiri) dominate the landscape and make a good challenge

# TREFOR, LLŶN PENINSULA, WALES

## A paddle of cliffs, choughs and childhood sweethearts

There are extraordinary views of the Llŷn Peninsula from the small Welsh village of Trefor, developed through its links with the local granite quarry. Its small harbour was a hive of activity in the days when stone was shipped all over the world. Nowadays, the inner harbour is mostly occupied by small fishing and pleasure boats. It is also a popular launch spot for paddlers looking to explore the dramatic north coast of the Llŷn.

Launching from Trefor harbour, a relaxed stand up paddle to Nant Gwrtheyrn, is a journey that never fails to deliver. Heading out westwards from the harbour you'll soon find yourself below some impressive sea cliffs with stacks, small caves and puffing blow holes ... all of which sit within the shadow of the rather impressive 'Yr Eifl' standing at 1,841 feet (562m) – one of the peaks that dominate the north coast of the Llŷn.

The beaches and hidden coves along this stretch are steep and bouldery, which makes landing on a SUP at times a little tricky. They are certainly worth exploring as many have possessed hidden treasures brought in on storm surges – past finds have included messages in bottles and unusual fishing buoys that have drifted in from foreign lands.

Nant Gwrtheyrn poses a magical eeriness, a once thriving mining village that was abandoned and now steeped in myths and haunting tales. One of the most famous tales is that of childhood sweethearts 'Rhys and Meinir', who still haunt the village to this very day. From the beach you can climb the steep steps to visit the language centre and be rewarded with a locally made ice cream or a beer from the café.

The Wales Coastal Path passes through Trefor – arguably this stretch is one of the most scenic and beautiful stretches of the 870-mile (1,400km) path as it winds its way over the cliff tops generously offering breathtaking views across the Irish Sea. Walkers often wave and take photographs when you paddle on the waters beneath them.

The spring tides for most of this section are never much more than 2 knots (3.7kph). The north of the Llŷn can be exposed to any winds with a north or westerly element, it is best to paddle with southeasterlies forecast, where you will receive shelter from the sea cliffs.

This journey can be made either as an A-B, with a car left at the end point at Nant Gwrtheyrn (NB there is a steep climb up to the car park), or made as a return journey using the tides for assistance. This paddle can also be continued further along the coast to Nefyn or Porthdinllaen. Wild camping is not permitted anywhere in Wales – there are lots of high-quality campsites and accommodation offers nearby.

Expect to see a vast array of wildlife in and around Trefor, but particularly do keep an eye out for the distinctive Red Legged Choughs (Brân Goesgoch) that ride the coastal air currents and nest in the cliff top crevices. When on the water keep an eye out for passing pods of dolphins (Dolffin) and porpoise (Llamhidydd).

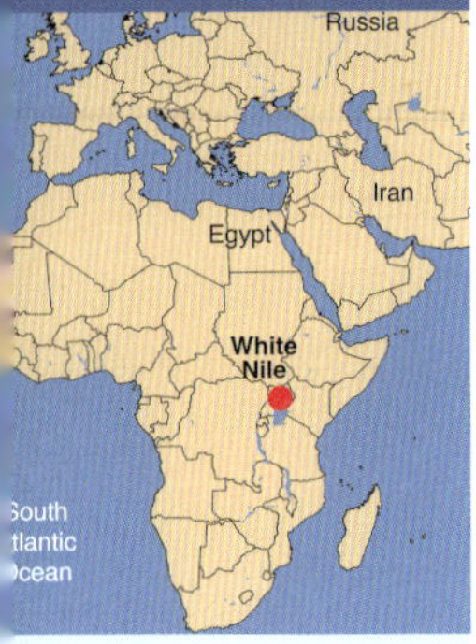


**Grade**
4-4+

**Experience**
Intermediate

**Getting there**
Fly to the international airport at Entebbe and then take a taxi, or minibus (matatus) to the town of Jinja or one of the camps at Bujagali Falls. To get back after you've run the river take a boda boda (moped). Whistling along jungle tracks with your kayak across your lap while you hang on to the driver for dear life is scarier than the river itself!

**In this location**
The White Nile should have enough water to satisfy any enthusiast

**On land**
Uganda boasts a wealth of wildlife and tours to see its mountain gorillas are popular. Alternatively, a day or two spent helping at one of the local 'soft power' projects, building or helping out in local schools is a good way to give something back for all the fun that you've had on the river

# THE WHITE NILE, UGANDA

## Surfing the source – the massive rapids of the mighty White Nile

Despite its troubled and violent past, modern day Uganda has moved from beneath the shadow of former dictator Idi Amin to become a successful and prosperous east African nation. It also has the White Nile flowing through its lush, green land. The White Nile was first discovered by John Hanning Speke in 1862. Speke was an English explorer and the first European to reach Lake Victoria, which he correctly identified as the long-sought source of the Nile. He would have been amazed if he'd known that in the future the crashing chaos of the river's huge rapids would become a playground to people in small brightly coloured plastic boats and rubber rafts.

The section of river that flows right from the Owen Falls Dam at the source is a magnet to whitewater 'playboaters'. These intrepid souls run the massive whitewater rapids and surf some of the biggest standing waves on the planet as they carve and bounce in to impressive aerial moves. This section of the Nile is also popular with rafters and a thriving tourist economy has grown up around this in the town of Jinja and the nearby Bujagali Falls, with some companies even running riverside camps complete with bars and accommodation. It attracts adventurers from all over the world, even British royalty (Prince William ran the White Nile in a raft).

The river is braided and flows in a series of channels. Some hide amazing rapids and super waves; others hide their own watery versions of hell. The main rapids that are regularly run are big, but the overall nature of the river is friendly, it's a Big Friendly African Giant if you will, and the warm water and large flat sections at the end of each rapid mean that a trashing and swim usually ends up OK. The runnable section is usually divided into two separate 'day' sections and these are split by three channels that hide some of the biggest and gnarliest drops on the river. Itanda is long and drawn out and many a rafter or kayaker has endured the beating of their lives at its hand. It's so big that even its individual features have their own names. The Cuban (it'll light you up), the Ash Tray (it'll stub you out), the Bad Place (needs no explanation), The Other Place (that's where you'll go if you end up in here): the names say it all. The other channels are home to Kalagala, a hugely powerful waterfall that makes kayakers look like tiny bits of driftwood as they run it; and Hypoxia, a rapid so big that it's only been run a handful of times and only by those with big lungs and bigger 'coconuts'.

The infrastructure around the river, the warm and friendly people (Uganda's real treasure), and the forgiving nature of the White Nile make it a brilliant 'Big Water' adventure destination for all abilities.

**Experience**
Intermediate

**Getting there**
It's easy to fly direct to Morocco from most places in Europe and get straight into the heart of the action. If you're coming from further afield you may need to transfer

**In this location**
Surf kayaking is the name of the game, but there's so many diverse breaks you'll need several trips to really begin to scratch the surface. Hire a 4x4 vehicle and go explore

**On land**
Spending a day exploring the Kasbah in Agadir is time well spent, but be prepared to do some serious, but good-natured, haggling. There is also some great mountain biking in the area and it's possible to hire good quality bikes and guides. But for the ultimate Morocco diversion, why not try a camel ride?

# MOROCCO

## Surfing under the crescent moon

The north African Kingdom of Morocco has been a well-known surf destination for many years now, home to plenty of board surfers, searching for that perfect wave. But the breaks of Morocco also offer superb surf kayaking experience with warm water, uncrowded surf spots, friendly locals and an exotic and exciting culture to add that extra dash of spice.

The waves are primarily firing and consistent later in the year, which makes it a good autumn or winter destination. Morocco is also the land of the point break, and the coast around the Agadir area is literally overflowing with fantastic surf spots. With so many great breaks on offer it means that, even with the annual influx of travelling surfers, the waves and line-ups are usually blissfully quiet. It's also a destination that will reward the adventurous and those prepared to load their surf kayaks onto a 4X4 and head south from Agadir will be blessed with some breathtaking surfing, possibly on virgin waves that have never borne a surf craft before.

Taghazout is one of the best known surfing areas and a well-known winter surf trip for visiting

surfers, which means it has lost a little of its local flavour over the last few decades. Anchor Point is the main break in the region and when it's pumping you'll find yourself screaming down big, heavy aqua blue wave faces, the chop thundering under your hull and blood rushing through your brain as you race to make the section as it begins to tube overhead! Get it right and you'll be screaming with exhilaration, get it wrong and you'll feel the ocean's might.

There are also a myriad of other breaks. Mysteries, Dog Steps, Hash Point, The Source and Killer Point are all home to some of the best waves in Morocco not to mention all those spots waiting to be discovered. It all comes down to what type of wave you fancy and what's working with the incoming swells.

It's easy to become intoxicated by the heady mix that Morocco offers and get lost in the rhythm of the surfing life. Rise early, surf, eat, drink mint tea, surf, head into the nearest village or town to visit a souk, maybe buy a rug, and to enjoy a mouth-watering meal cooked in a traditional tagine or a delectable local fresh fish dish. Then head back to your apartment to sleep before a new day and you're doing it all again.

The flavours of Morocco are varied and rich, just like its waves and it's certainly a surf dish that once tasted will have you craving your next helping of surfing in the land of the crescent moon.

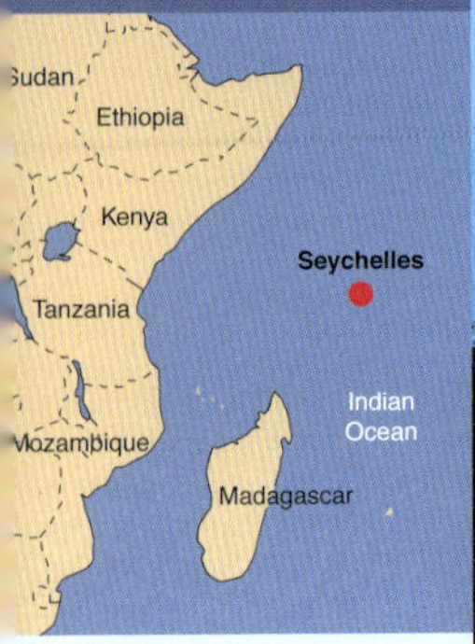

**Experience**
Novice

**Getting there**
The main gateway airport is Seychelles International at Mahe. Air Seychelles is the main carrier, offering direct flights from India, Israel, Malaysia, Singapore, South Africa and Thailand

**In this location**
Island hopping is the name of the game in this tropical paradise. To avoid long crossings, you can also take an inter-island ferry from Mahé to Praslin

**On land**
The islands of Mahé and Praslin have numerous hiking trails worth exploring, especially Praslin's Valléé de Mai, one of the Seychelles' two World Heritage Sites, that takes you through a forest of more than 6,000 Coco de Mer trees thought to be the original Garden of Eden

# SEYCHELLES

## Paddling in Eden

If you threw a dart at a globe hoping it would land on a tropical paradise for paddling, you couldn't do much better than the Seychelles, an archipelago of 115 granite and coral islands off the east coast of Africa, just north of Madagascar. Described as 'a string of pearls set in the azure waters of the Indian Ocean', the island chain is scripted for sea kayaking, snorkelling and siestas under palm trees.

While the islands are inhabited by 100,000 or so people (most of whom speak English and / or French, or native Creole), the majority live on the three inner islands of Mahé, Praslin and La Digue, leaving the rest of the archipelago in unspoilt splendour for sea kayaking. Boasting everything from exotic wildlife to clear blue seas, and warm waters for snorkelling, each island has its own disposition; from hillsides draped in lush jungles to beaches lined with massive granite cliffs and sculpted boulders found nowhere else in the world.

Because of their small size and close proximity, kayaking between the islands is easy, allowing for flexible paddling itineraries.

One place to start is by circumnavigating the island of Praslin, the Seychelles' second-largest inhabited island. Head clockwise around the island's eastern, southern and western coasts and you'll

get an up close and personal view of its unique pink granite formations. You can also stop at Anse Possession, a cove named for the 'Stone of Possession' placed by French explorers more than 200 years ago.

Another hotspot is the island of La Digue, which houses even more impressive rock formations and beaches. Its coastline allows you to poke your bow into nooks and crannies, and land on pristine beaches for snorkelling sessions, beachcombing and lunch caught from the sea. After resting, you can head to the granite of Coco Island, which offers perhaps the best snorkelling on the archipelago, thanks to its rocky shelves serving as a safe hold for tropical fish. Next, continue on to Grande Soeur and the islands of Curieuse and Aride, a protected reserve home to more native bird species than anywhere else in the Seychelles. It also harbours a tortoise conservation farm where you can learn everything you want to about these denizens of the deep.

For additional birding, Cousine Island also houses a bird sanctuary protected as a national park. Tortoises come with its territory also, with 350 living on the island at last count. Other paddling options include La Digue Island, 'the land that time forgot' with beaches framed by large boulders; and the Coco Islands, which are famous for their coral reefs.

To make logistics easier, many paddlers base camp out of sailboats (charted out of Mahé), letting you drop anchor at night and sail to whatever island suits your sea kayaking fancy each day. 16 of the islands offer some sort of lodging accommodations, from five-star lodges to quaint bungalows. The islands are also free from malaria and other tropical diseases, with no vaccinations required for visiting.

**Grade**
1-5

**Experience**
Intermediate – Expert

**Getting there**
Most people access Augrabies by flying from Cape Town to the airport in Upington. From there, it's a 78-mile (126km) drive to the park

**In this location**
For a four-day canoe trip, head to the mountainous desert region of Richtersveldt National Park, basing out of Vioolsdrift. Here, you can canoe quiet waters in wilderness solitude, camping on the shore the entire way

**On land**
Several hiking trails exist in the park, as well as overlooks providing views of Augrabies Falls. Plan some time out of your boat to take in the sights. If you're in South Africa, take some time for a wildlife safari

# ORANGE RIVER, SOUTH AFRICA

## Adventure on the Augrabies

For remote paddling Africa-style, try the Orange River in South Africa's Northern Cape as it plunges through Augrabies Falls National Park, one of the most isolated areas of the country.

The 1,350-mile-long (2,172km) Orange River, the longest in South Africa, begins in the Drakensberg mountains in Lesotho before flowing west to the Atlantic Ocean. En route, it forms part of the international borders between South Africa and Namibia, and between South Africa and Lesotho. While it also provides water for irrigation and hydro power – its Gariep Dam is the largest in the country – its allure for paddling is as strong as ever.

The game-rich region was once a haven for outlaws and other renegades. Today paddlers come for the same wilderness and solitude. One of the most popular regions for paddling is Augrabies Falls National Park, which lies 78 miles (126km) west of the town of Upington, the starting-off point for most excursions into the park.

Meaning the 'Noise-Making Place' for the thunderous roar of its cascades, Augrabies Falls plunges 165 feet (50m) into a 10-mile-long (16km) canyon of brilliant red rock the colour of the setting sun. Whitewater buffs target the section below the falls, between the Ararat and Echo Corner view sites, where big-water, Class 4-5 rapids comparable to those on the mighty Zambezi careen through the gorge. The section offers several intermediary public access points to its frothy drops. For those wanting less adrenaline, there are also five miles (8km) of Class 2-3 rapids above the falls, suitable for whitewater kayaks and rafts.

The Orange also boasts plenty of canoeing options. Four day-long routes in the vicinity trace 35 miles (56km) of the river's calm-water sections, which boast great scenery and gentle Class 1-2 rapids. You can also take a half-day trip in canoes or inflatable kayaks from Upington to Oukamp.

For accommodations inside the park you can choose from self-catering chalets and bed & breakfasts to a variety of camping options, most of which lie a few miles outside of the park. Lodges can be found 25 miles (40km) north-west in Kakamas.

Because temperatures during the rainy season (January to April) can reach 46°C (115°F), most paddlers head there in the cooler months of April to September, when flows are perfect for the river's canoeing stretches as well as world-class whitewater. Whenever you go, prepare for a true diamond in the rough – literally. In 1867, the Eureka Diamond, the first diamond discovered in South Africa, was found near Hopetown along the river. Two years later, the larger Star of South Africa diamond was found in the same region.

**Experience**
Expert

**Getting there**
Situated in northern Zimbabwe on the Zambezi River, far from any major town, Mana Pools is remote. To get there, fly to Harare and then drive or arrange other ground transportation along the main Harare/Chirundu road. At the bottom of the Zambezi Escarpment, veer onto a dirt road that will take you 43 miles (70km) to the Nyamepi Camp

**In this location**
You can string together longer trips from Kariba to Chirundu, Chirundu to Kanyemba, or an eight-day trip from Kariba to Kanyemba

**On land**
Hire a park guide to go on a tracking expedition at dawn. Visitors can join park staff as they track radio-collared lions on foot, assisting in data collection for various research projects

# MANA POOLS NATIONAL PARK, ZIMBABWE

## Wildlife wonderland

If you want to canoe with wildlife, set your compass bearings on Zimbabwe's Mana Pools National Park and the lower Zambezi River. Meaning 'four' in the local Shona dialect, referring to four large permanent pools formed by the river: the region is one of Africa's best game-viewing areas. As the outlying lakes dry up, game gravitates to the pools, drawing wildlife in droves.

There's no better way to experience the wildlife than from the seat of a canoe, which lets you traverse its 965 square miles (2,500km$^2$) of river frontage under forests of mahogany, wild figs, ebonies and baobab trees. Rated one of the best parks in Africa, the park owes itself to the Zambezi River, which defines the boundary between Zimbabwe and Zambia. To the river's north rise the mountains of Zambia, capping the African landscape.

But its real vistas are its animals – which can also be the main detriment to canoeing and camping if you're not careful. Unless you're familiar with the ins and outs of canoeing in Africa (the habits of its predators), consider going with a local outfitter, which will save you the regulatory logistical headaches of going privately. Even if you decide to go alone, consider hiring a guide, who can bring invaluable knowledge and insight, from teaching you how to track animals, to how to avoid them. Located nearly

500 miles (805km) downstream from the Zambezi's upper whitewater reaches near Victoria Falls, the river here is tranquil. But there's still plenty of current – almost 30,000 cubic feet (850m$^3$) per second in the dry season – to help you progress downstream. You can take day trips from base camps or lodges, or piece together longer itineraries.

If you're venturing out into the bush, bear the animals in mind: there are plenty of them to both see and steer clear of. One of the least developed parks in southern Africa, Mana Pools has the country's largest concentration of hippos and crocodiles, both of which should be given a wide berth. Hippos, in particular, need to be treated with respect. Get between one and the water and you can get trampled; get too close in the water and you can get charged (stay close together in narrow side channels).

The region also has large populations of elephant, Cape buffalo, rhinos, zebra, giraffe and waterbuck, as well as such predators as hyenas, lions, leopards, cheetahs and more.

In short, it's a wildlife wonderland. Leave one animal in your wake and another appears off your bow. Tourist facilities in the park include five riverside lodges where you can view wildlife at sunset. The lodges make great base camps for daily canoe outings. The park also has communal and private campsites, including the group Nyamepi Camp along the river. More exclusive sites offer solitude and come with braai stands and toilet facilities.

The park is only open to cars during the dry season; during the rainy season you have to travel by foot or by boat. The best time to visit is from May to early September, with the best game viewing lasting until late October (but October is also the hottest). Most companies offer canoe safaris from April to November.

WHITEWATER

**Grade**
3-5

**Experience**
Intermediate – Expert

**Getting there**
There are many options by air, the easiest is to fly to Johannesburg in South Africa, then on to Livingstone. In Livingstone there are several raft firms and kayak schools who can help with logistics and porters

**In this location**
The Minus rapids between Victoria Falls and the Boiling Pot put-in are a challenge for the best paddlers and below Rapid 24 there are several days of good quality Zambezi-style whitewater to enjoy

**On land**
Zambia is a beautiful country with lots to do: fishing, safaris and even bungee jumping are just a few of the incredible activities that can be enjoyed

# ZAMBEZI RIVER, AFRICA

## Wham, bam, thank you Zam!

The Zambezi, known by many kayakers simply as the Zam, is the fourth longest river in Africa, rising in Zambia before flowing through four countries and then emptying into the Indian Ocean. The section that interests kayakers the most starts just below the world-famous Victoria Falls and flows down through 24 named rapids, each with their own character and challenges. The water level of the Zambezi fluctuates depending on the time of year: in spring the Zam reaches its highest flows producing monumental waves and rapids to scare even the bravest and adrenaline-crazed kayakers; in the last few months of the year the water levels are at their lowest and the Zambezi is at its steepest.

All the big rapids on the Zambezi have been named; the put-in is known as the Boiling Pot, the Zambezi thunders down through the Minus rapids below Victoria Falls and explodes into huge pulsing mushrooms of water, known as boils by kayakers because the water behaves as if it was being boiled! The Zambezi's three most famous rapids are Number Nine – Commercial Suicide, Number 11 – Overland Truck Eater and Number 12b – the most famous surfing wave on the whole river. Commercial Suicide is a crazy mess of huge breaking waves – the longer you spend looking for a line through the rapid the more intimidating the challenge becomes. Overland Truck Eater is one of the most iconic waves on the Zambezi, for about two weeks per year a huge tubing wave forms. The best kayakers are able to surf their kayaks inside the tube. This is a unique wave, tubing waves are hardly ever found on whitewater rivers. Number 12b forms for the last third of the year and provides quite simply one of the best river waves for kayaking in the world, many new kayak freestyle moves have been invented and developed here.

A trip to the Zambezi will be remembered as a trip of a lifetime, the huge waves and rapids will bring a beaming smile to your face for years after you run them and the stories of monstrous breaking waves and death defying lines between will entertain your paddling buddies every time you tell them. Kayaking in Africa is always an adventure and a trip down the Zambezi is one of the best kayaking adventures the continent of Africa has to offer.

**Experience**
Intermediate

**Getting there**
From the capital Vientiane, make you way to Luang Prabang by bus, train or plane. From here there are daily bus services to Sam Neua, the provincial capital in the north-east. This will take you to Vieng Kham (5-7 bumpy hours), the start of this descent

**In this location**
Laos is criss-crossed with beautiful rivers, many of which end up in the Mekong. Multiple large dam projects currently disturb the wildlife and local people, but there are still lots of sections to discover. It's better to paddle after the monsoon for the best conditions and cool temperatures (October to January)

**On land**
Enjoy a stop in Luang Prabang. The ancient capital is full of temples, museums and restaurants, so spend an evening on the banks of the Mekong enjoying the golden sunset and sampling the street food. Learn about the local cultures such as the Hmong people and the fallout from the Secret War

# NAM SUANG & SENG RIVERS, LAOS

## An epic journey down Laos' secret rivers

This epic journey down 90 miles (140km) of unspoilt river in northern Laos will give you a glimpse of traditional life on the banks of the jungle at a calm pace. The green wall of trees and creepers is the perfect backdrop as the Nam Suang and Seng rivers meander peacefully through the sprawling mountains. It is easy paddling, mostly class 1 with a few class 2 sections. There is one harder rapid (class 3) on the final leg 12 miles (20km) before arriving on the Mekong. It can be portaged on river right both on the bank or on the road further up. There is a constant current that will help you along, but expect to paddle continuously to keep going, especially on the upper portion where there is less water.

The track on river right follows the entire descent, which can be reassuring for those that are not used to multi-day paddles in the jungle and provides a simple exit route in case of emergency. There are also plenty of small villages, that increase in size towards the end of the trip, with the possibility of getting extra supplies.

Getting to Vieng Kham can be an adventure in itself, and would be practically impossible with a hardshell boat. The small market is perfect for some last provisions or a meal, and a small path leads down to the river beneath the main bridge. Inflate your packrafts and paddle off into the forest! This trip alternates wild sections where your only companions are the birds and other wildlife you may have the

chance to encounter, and small villages. Keep your eyes open for a flash of blue that heralds a kingfisher flying low across the water!

As you traverse the small hamlets you will probably be greeted by the children that play on the banks. Their parents meanwhile are busy fishing, farming or panning for gold on the sandy beaches. They can also be seen mending the home-made hydroelectric generators used to power small appliances such as phone chargers. You will have to paddle around them and also pass beneath makeshift bamboo bridges, rebuilt every year after the monsoon floods. Other telltale signs of the river's power can be seen in the debris stuck in the branches high above.

There are plenty of beaches and coves to pitch a tent and spend the night. If you keep away from the villages you will be left on your own and can enjoy the sounds of the forest. It can get quite chilly and damp in the winter months though thankfully there is an abundance of dry drift wood for campfires. Mornings are often grey, but the hot sun soon burns off the morning fog. The Nam Seng finally enters the Mekong, 0.93 miles (1.5km) above Luang Prabang. The scenery changes dramatically, opening up and the river stretches far out into the distance. This huge expanse of water will take you all the way to the city and the end of the trip.

The descent can be accomplished in roughly six days depending on how many hours you want to paddle and water levels, that will drop slowly after the floods. If you fancy a shorter trip, you could consider getting a driver to drop you off on the lower section or try the Nam Khan river that also arrives in Luang Prabang. If you are feeling adventurous you could bikeraft this itinerary too.

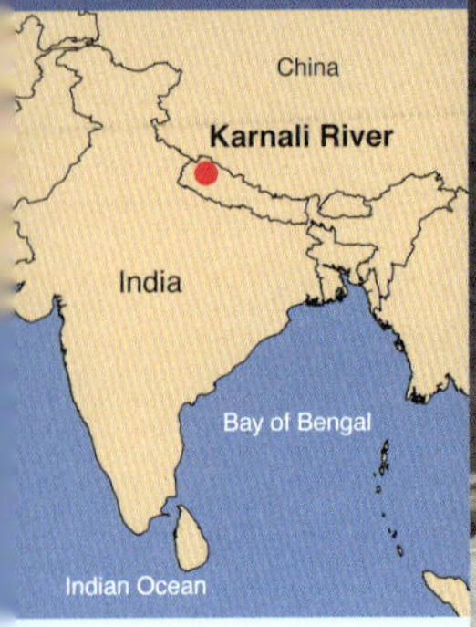


**Grade**
3-6

**Experience**
Expert

**Getting there**
Fly to Katmandu then get a bus to Pohkara, then on to Nepalgunj and then an aeroplane to Simikot. You will need your passport to fly to Simikot

**In this location**
Nepal is a premier destination for whitewater adventuring with more rivers and adventures than you can imagine. There are many superb paddling adventures accessible from Pohkara

**On land**
Nepal offers many degrees of land-based entertainment, from a day out to the Monkey Temple in Katmandu or a trek to Everest base camp, there is something for everyone

# KARNALI RIVER, NEPAL

## Adventure beyond belief – every aspect is a challenge

Hiding out in the wild west of Nepal is the Karnali River, widely regarded as one of the best multi-day whitewater kayaking expeditions in the world. To completely descend the 248 miles (400km) of the Karnali River most teams need about two weeks and will be faced with long, technical rapids up to Grade 5 in difficulty, some of which must be portaged around, remote jungle that is home to crocodiles, snakes and panthers, and local Nepalese people who have seldom travelled away from their home villages. The Karnali River is an incredible adventure; the upper Humla Karnali has only been descended by a few intrepid teams whereas the lower section can be enjoyed as part of a commercial rafting tour.

Just getting to the put-in Simikot is an ultimate adventure; first a 14-hour bus ride from Pohkara to Nepalgunj and then you must arrange a light aeroplane to fly you, your team and your kayaks up to Simikot, probably one of the scariest places to land an aeroplane in the world! With two weeks' worth of food and expedition equipment loaded into your kayak it is very heavy and the easiest way to get it all

down the narrow track from Simikot village to the put-in is to hire a local porter to carry it down for you.

Once on the water the real adventure starts; the Karnali starts off with easy read-and-run rapids surrounded by a fantastic landscape. As the valley turns into a gorge the rapids become progressively harder and harder until on the third day a series of very complex rapids challenge the team. The risk of running these rapids is simply too great and it is necessary to carry the heavy kayaks over land until the river eases off enough to allow the team back onto the water. The 0.93-mile (1.5km) portage over challenging terrain with all the equipment takes a whole day.

The middle section of the Karnali is simply superb, 155 miles (250km) of big volume whitewater with committing rapids and fair lines; multi-day whitewater kayaking does not get any better. The hardest section is the last section to the road bridge in Chisapani, 62 miles (100km) of flat water. This section is just hard work paddling towards a point where it is possible to get off the river and get a bus back to Pohkara, a warm shower, a steak and cold beer and then a real bed!

The Karnali is an incredible adventure that will challenge even the best teams of whitewater adventurers, every aspect of your skills will be tested, from bargaining a fair price for fresh fish or chicken to supplement the expedition rations of rice and instant noodles, to paddling very challenging whitewater rapids in the wilderness of western Nepal. Along the way you will meet many friendly people, curious children and experience some of the best, most challenging days of your life, and in 50 years you will tell stories your grandchildren will struggle to believe!

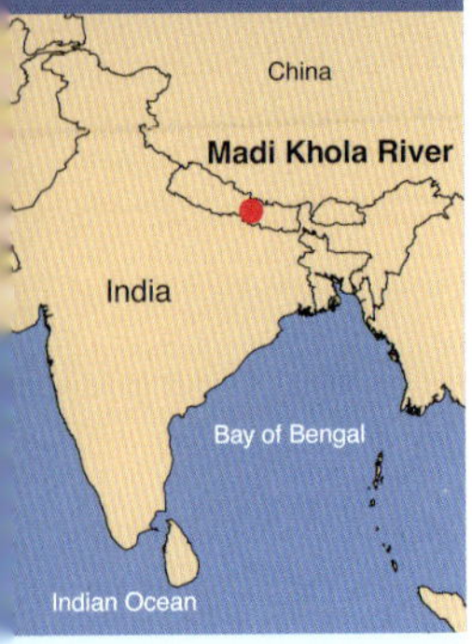


**Grade**
4-5

**Experience**
Expert

**Getting there**
Fly in to Kathmandu, Nepal's capital, and then take a bus or taxi to Pokhara. From there it is easy to arrange transport, permits and porters with one of the local rafting or trekking operators

**In this location**
If the Madi Khola is your cup of chai then the Modi Khola and the Marsyangdi rivers are also going to provide excellent sport

**On land**
The Madi is only a stone's throw away from the main Annapurna trekking route. Pokhara is an outdoor enthusiast's dream and you can arrange trekking, climbing and mountain biking trips from there. It's also bustling with great places to eat, hotels and bars

# MADI KHOLA RIVER, NEPAL

## Non-stop adrenaline-fuelled whitewater adventure

The mountain kingdom of Nepal has long held a place in the hearts of river-running whitewater kayakers and its mountain valleys are home to some of the best multi-day rivers in the world. Many of Nepal's great rivers are of the big volume, huge wave variety but nestled over in the Annapurna range is the Madi Khola, a beautiful and remote mountain stream that offers steep boulder gardens and pushy whitewater to test the thrill-seeking whitewater adventurer.

The base from which to embark on a Madi trip is Nepal's second city of Pokhara, where you can arrange your transport and porters for the trek in. You can get to the start of the trail leading to the Madi by using a local taxi, if you can find one with a roof rack, but it's better to hire a jeep that can get you and your kayak further up the trail. As you bump along a riverbed with water splashing all around it already feels like a mini-expedition. When the jeeps have reached the trailhead it's time to shoulder the backpacks, give the kayaks to the porters and hit the trail. Kayakers are usually, by nature, a self-sufficient breed, so it may feel a little odd to have someone else carrying your boat. But for the local porters it is a way of life and how they make a living to provide for their families, so it's important to contribute to the local economy as much as possible.

As you climb the trail the sheer beauty of the place will overcome you. The Annapurna glisten in the bright blue sky above and tempting glimpses of the river glitter from within the steep-sided gorge below. You may even see the local honey hunters hanging from cliffs as they gather honey from huge combs that are made by giant cliff bees. Finally you'll reach the village of Souda and this is where most river trips start from, although it is possible to go higher still. Once afloat on the Madi Khola it just doesn't stop, continuous clean, sweet rapids one on top of another for hours on end.

At the end of that first day, you can camp at the river's edge, or stay at a riverside tea house where you can enjoy a tray of dhal bhat washed down with gallons of sweet black chai, before lying awake all night buzzing off the day's excitement and the huge amount of sugar you've imbibed with the tea!

The following morning you'll rise under the shadow of towering and majestic Himalayan giants, before once again enjoying a day of non-stop, exhilarating whitewater action. The journey's end lies at Karputar where you'll emerge from the river wide-eyed and grinning like a mad man from your marvellous Madi experience.

**Experience**
Novice

**Getting there**
Phuket is about 400 miles (643km) south of Bangkok Zat at the southern end of the Isthmus of Kra in the Indian Ocean. A launch from any point along its east coast takes you into Phang Nga Bay

**In this location**
Believe it or not, the lush Phang Nga Province also offers several rafting options, a few of which take you through the Ton Pariwat Wildlife Sanctuary

**On land**
Well, you'll actually be a bit above land, but if you're in Phuket you might as well take a ride on an elephant through the jungle and tour a rubber plantation (it's a national symbol of Thailand)

# PHANG NGA BAY, THAILAND

## A licence to thrill – sea kayaking in sea caves

Unleash your inner James Bond by grabbing a sit-on-top kayak and heading to the karst islands of Phuket, Thailand. Here you'll find towering, limestone columns rising straight out of Phang Nga Bay, water-filled caves (hongs in Thai) that will have you leaning back in your boat, and passages so narrow you'll have to place your paddle alongside your craft. All this comes with tropical beaches and gin-clear water (shaken, not stirred) that would give even 007 pause from his mission.

Koh Ta-pu, the rocky-pinnacled island that starred in Bond's *The Man With the Golden Gun* is located there, as are such islands as Koh Hong and Koh Panyi (Sea Gypsy Island), which harbours storefronts on stilts and a Muslim fishing village.

Because of its climate and caves, most people tour the area in either inflatable kayaks or sit-upons – they let you hop off easily when the going gets tight or you need to cool off. Another piece of mandatory equipment is a waterproof flashlight so you can take in everything from the caves' stalactites ('t' means they come from the top) and oozing flowstones. More than 160 islands lie scattered throughout the

bay, harbouring jungle-lined cliffs, bluffs and overhangs. Most are made of limestone, whose calcium carbonate makes them conducive to caves ... thousands of them, whose egress varies with the tide. Hit them when it's too high and they'll be buried; too low and you might not be able to get in. Consider hiring a local guide who knows their ins and outs (try Sea Cave Canoe).

Many of the islands also harbour secret lagoons and beaches, some of which are accessed by paddling through caves. Some of the larger islands let you paddle up estuaries and other nooks and explore large forests of mangrove. The island of Khao Khien near Koh Panyi also offers the chance to see ancient paintings of boats and animals on its sheer rock walls, all from the seat of your kayak.

There's plenty of animal life as well. You'll see (and hear) everything from monkeys swinging from the branches to butterflies, birds and more in the jungle, and below your hull you'll view sponges, jellyfish, sea urchins and coral. Lift your hat brim to the sky and you might even see an endangered white-bellied sea eagle, whose six-foot (1.8m) wingspan almost eclipses the length of your paddle.

Regardless of where you go, give it more than a day; there's just too much to see and too many islands and caves to explore. One good place to stay is the island of Koh Panyi, which offers bungalows and a variety of local restaurants. While there aren't many regulations concerning paddling in the area (for both private paddlers and commercial operations), check with a local outfitter for conditions and advice before heading out; chances are you won't have Q watching your back like he does James Bond.

**Experience**
Novice

**Getting there**
Fly into Vietnam's capital of Hanoi and either rent a car or hire a driver to take you to your base out of Hạ long City

**In this location**
Head down to Ho Chi Minh City/Saigon to paddle the narrow channels and floating markets and villages of the Mekong River

**On land**
Take a traditional cyclo (pedicab) tour of Hanoi, Vietnam's capital. Hot spots include the Old Quarter, Hoàn Kiếm Lake, the Ho Chi Minh mausoleum and traditional stilt house, the One-Pillar Pagoda, and such temples as Quán Thánh and Trấn Quốc Pagoda along West Lake. Also make time to tour the Ngọc Sơn Temple in the middle of Hoan Kiem Lake, which is idyllic for a moonlit paddle

# HẠ LONG BAY, VIETNAM

## A surreal experience with magical scenery

The most famous place to sea kayak in Vietnam is also the bay most steeped in legend.

According to local lore, in ancient times a giant dragon threw itself into Hạ Long Bay, creating thousands of islands with the flick of his tail.

Whether the dragon origins are true or not, there's no denying that the results of either the tail-flick or geology have created waters sprinkled with tropical islands that are sculpted perfectly for paddling. Thousands of limestone karsts and islands dot the bay's aquamarine waters, offering paddlers the chance to explore hidden coves, sea caves, lagoons and unspoilt beaches, all while hopping from isle to isle. The scattered islands also keep the water calm, making the region perfect for everyone from beginners to experts.

Perhaps the area's best attraction for sea kayakers are its sea caves, carved out of the islands' limestone into giant arches, passages and tunnels. You'll be hard pressed to find more sea caves squeezed into such a small area anywhere on the planet.

Of course, culture is every bit as much a part of the package as the area's sea caves and pristine paddling. En route you can paddle up to traditional floating fishing villages, explore temples and other ceremonial sites, and even overnight, if so you desire, in a traditional wooden junk as a mother ship (hire a captain out of Hạ Long Bay).

Most trips originate out of Hạ Long Bay, which is a short drive via the ceramic village of Bát Tràng from Hanoi (note: you'll likely drive atop the dike along the Red River delta). If exploring ancient temples is your cup of tea, there's plenty of that along the way as well before you hit the water.

One of south-east Asia's premier tourist destinations, Hạ Long Bay is best seen from the water, and one of the most intimate ways to do so is from the seat of a kayak. Van Gio Island is a popular first stop, with a secluded beach for a swim and snorkel. From there you can access a string of islands littered with coves and sea caves. One of the most beautiful islands is Bo Han where you will find Luon Cave. Paddle through its arc-shaped entrance and you will be in the middle of a small jade-green water lake. There you can glimpse towering limestone mountains and sometimes catch sight of many friendly golden monkeys.

Other hotspots to mark on your map are Ba Men, a beachside temple dedicated to the whale gods (you can paddle right up to it and even camp nearby); and mile-long (1.6km) Hanh Cave near Cẩm Phả . If time allows, also steer your rudder toward Bai Tu Long, billed as one of the world's most beautiful bays. Other caves to put on your itinerary include Trinh Nữ, Đầu Gỗ and Thiên Cung.

**Experience**
Intermediate – Expert

**Getting there**
Peron Peninsula is located 480 miles (772km) north of Perth. The best way to get there is by air, flying into the Shark Bay Airport, or by road via the World Heritage Drive, a 93-mile (150km) road between Denham and the Overlander Roadhouse on the North-West Coastal Highway

**In this location**
That's about it in that neck of the woods, save for the more exposed coastline. But plenty of other sea kayaking options abound near Perth, which offer proximity to a large population base

**On land**
Check out the new Discovery & Visitor Centre in Denham, which provides interactive displays and other information about the region and World Heritage Site, as well as the historical Peron Homestead. If you have the time, check out the Monkey Mia Dolphin Resort

# PERON PENINSULA & SHARK BAY, AUSTRALIA

## Outback adventuring Australia-style

You'll be saying 'G'day mate' aplenty paddling Western Australia's Peron Peninsula, located in the Shark Bay World Heritage Site.

Named for French naturalist François Péron, who first visited the area in 1801, the peninsula was purchased by the national government in 1990 and has since become a boon for outdoor recreation as a nature reserve. Running north-west and located between the towns of Geraldton and Carnarvon, Peron is the largest of Shark Bay's peninsulas, measuring some 80 miles (129km) in length. All that means plenty of paddling and camping options in the Australian outback.

Just remember you're far removed from the conveniences of more populated, urban paddling destinations. Located on the westernmost point of Australia, Shark Bay is about as remote as you can get. But there's a reward for its remoteness: a pristine paddling environment you won't find anywhere else, including gin-clear water for snorkelling, tranquil beaches for camping, and a wealth of wildlife. The main word of note: bring a hat, sunscreen and plenty of water. The main settlements include

Denham and Monkey Mia, a popular tourist resort, noted for its research centre on bottlenose dolphins (you'll likely see plenty from your kayak). Both towns are great spots to start your journey as you paddle north-west into Shark Bay Marine Park and the Hamelin Pool Marine Nature Reserve. As you head up towards Shell Beach at the narrowest section of the peninsula, between Nanga and Goulet Bluff, you'll notice what makes the place so special.

With an average depth of just 30 feet (9m), the region is littered with peninsulas and islands for exploring. But topping this are its flora and fauna. Located in the transition zone between three major climatic regions, the shallow depth beneath your hull is also home to the 1,400-square-mile (1,030km$^2$) Wooramel Seagrass Bank, the largest seagrass bank in the world. Included in its swaying blades is the largest number of seagrass species ever recorded in one place. Further illustrating the area's biological diversity, in the south end of the bay stromalites have been found that have been billed as harbouring the earliest signs of life on Earth.

The bay is also replete with indigenous wildlife. Joining the region's waterborne species, Bernier and Dorre islands in the north-west corner of the heritage area include some of the last remaining habitats of Australian mammals threatened with extinction. These islands and others are used as a release area for threatened species bred at Project Eden in François Péron National Park.

Lest you spend all your time looking down in the water or horizontally at the region's island wildlife, you'll also want to cast your eyes skywards every once in a while; the bay is lined with sheer limestone cliffs overlooking its shallow waters.

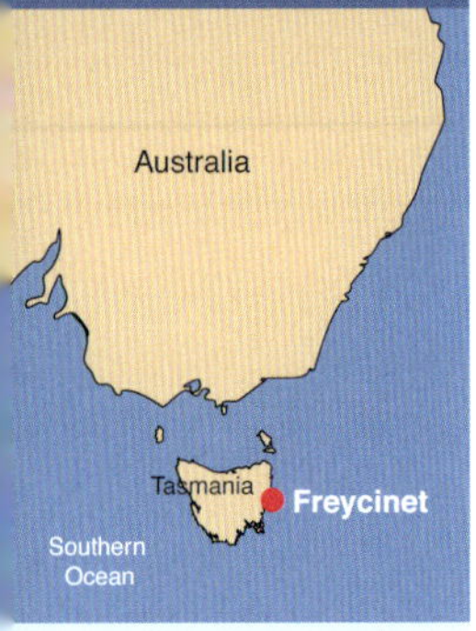


**Experience**
Intermediate – Expert

**Getting there**
From the capital of Hobart, it's a three-hour drive to Coles Bay where your trip starts, passing roadkill possum and eucalyptus trees all set against the sparkling Tasman Sea

**In this location**
If you have the time, fit in a multi-day rafting or kayaking trip down the World Heritage Site Franklin River

**On land**
You can also traverse the Hazards and hike to Wineglass Bay and beyond from Coles Bay

# FREYCINET NATIONAL PARK, TASMANIA, AUSTRALIA

## Tasmania's oldest National Park is a crown jewel

Paddling out from Coles Bay through Tasmania's Hazard Mountains in Freycinet National Park can give you sensory overload. The mountains' red granite complements turquoise waters, offering one of the most surreal sea kayaking experiences on the planet.

You won't be the first to notice it. On shore you'll see countless sand-covered mounds, or middens, whose shells are a result of eons of foraging by native Aborigines.

Though Tasmania has set aside 28 percent of its land as national parks, 46-square-mile ($119km^2$) Freycinet National Park, located halfway down the island's east coast, was the first, established in 1916. On the east side of the peninsula, 2,000-foot (610m) granite faces drop sheer to the Tasman Sea. On the west, protected waters let paddlers dip their blades unmolested, the spine of granite deflecting the majority of the prevailing wind skyward.

The region's climate and marine life also provides great habitat for flora and high-flying fauna. A third of Tasmania's plant species and half of its 230 bird species call the area home. Combined with its vibrant colours and calm waters, all this makes it some of the best sea kayaking in the southern hemisphere.

Campsites are often hidden in peely barked eucalyptus trees, where your kayaks' colours blend in with the bark's coloured streaks. As you sip local Chardonnay at sunset, whose pink clouds match the rose-coloured feldspar of the Hazard's granite, you can share stories of shipwrecked whalers and the region's early French explorers to the ocean's crescendos and cries of kookaburras and Tasmanian devils echoing across the water. Soon the southern ensemble will have you sound asleep.

Many people lay-over for a day or two to hike across the isthmus to Wineglass Bay, so named for its wide entrance narrowing to a stem before expanding again into a broad beach named one of world's top ten by *Outside* magazine. (Don't be surprised if you flush out a wallaby or two during the journey.) Made from eroded quartzite – the granite outcropping's weakest mineral – the beach is as picturesque as they come and the perfect place to spend an entire afternoon. A popular pastime: looking for New Zealand screw shells, a mollusc that threads into the sand to escape predators. While the bay resembled its wine-themed namesake better in earlier times when a nearby whaling station regularly filled it to the brim with the blood of southern rights, the station has been closed since 1840, leaving the bay and its beach pristine as nature intended.

Continue your paddle onward around Schouten Island or base camp where you are, touring amongst giant stingrays gliding effortlessly beneath your bow. Just keep an eye on the weather and remember that you're not far from Antarctica. And beware the afternoon Nor'easters. As the Tasmanian land mass heats up, the air over it rises and air from the Tasman Sea swoops in to fill the gap.

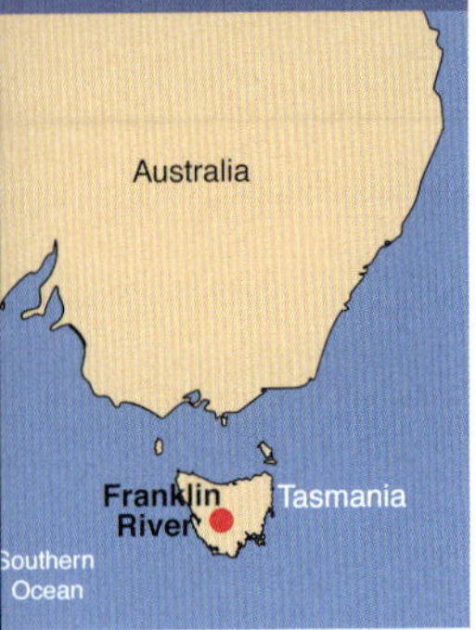


**Grade**
3-6

**Experience**
Expert

**Getting there**
Get yourself to Hobart, and from there arrange land transportation to the put-in as well as a return trip back from the take-out at Sir John Falls

**In this location**
Hobart offers several other whitewater day runs, including the Mersey (an hour drive from Launceton), Leven, Picton, Lea, Fisher, Broad, Nive and Butler's Gorge

**On land**
Hike to Kutikina Cave, an archaeological site that helped save the Franklin. It's believed to have housed the southernmost habitation of people during the last ice age, Aborigines who crossed from Australia before rising seas turned Tasmania into an island

# FRANKLIN RIVER, TASMANIA, AUSTRALIA

## A wilderness Eden – a river-running gem

A sign at the put-in for Tasmania's Franklin River reads, 'Warning: This is not the place to learn whitewater skills!'

It's sound advice. Best paddled from September to December, the 60-mile-long (97km) gorge takes most commercial raft trips 13 days to navigate, including four days to progress six miles (10km) through the Class 5-6 Great Ravine. Experienced kayakers, however, can run the waterway self-supported in four days, thanks to the ability to eddy-hop further downstream, making the portages easier.

But the river's wilderness is as much of a draw as its whitewater – and it has set a precedent for river conservation worldwide. In 1982, the government planned to dam the river, but backed off after the largest land-conservation rally in Australian history.

There was good reason for the uprising. The river is a wilderness gem, set in the midst of impenetrable rainforest and gorges in the island's south-west corner. Its rough terrain is largely why the British established penal settlements there, the most notorious of which was located at Macquarie Harbour, just downstream from the take-out.

Most parties put in on the Collingwood and bounce their way down to the Franklin, whose water is so clean you can drink it straight from the river. Filled with 1,000-year-old Huon pines and battalions of myrtle, sassafras, leatherwood, tea and laurel trees, the region's foliage, joined by tannin leeched from upstream buttongrass plains, gives the river its most unique feature: water the colour of tea. But keep your eye on the task at hand. Stories abound of the Franklin rising 10 feet (3m) in an hour, turning the portage-riddled Great Ravine into an eddyless maelstrom.

After navigating Finch's Crossing, proposed site of the first dam, you'll reach mile-long (1.6km) Irenabyss Gorge, meaning Chasm of Peace, where white tea tree flowers float like stars against the southern sky. As polished as a kitchen counter, the gorge's rock, Dolorite, is found only in Tasmania and parts of South America and Antarctica.

Next up: the Class 5-6 Great Ravine, including such sieve-filled rapids as The Churn, Coruscades and The Cauldron. At the biggest gauntlet is Thunder Rush, whose high portage (required at high flows) requires ten hours of hauling gear straight up and down above a roiling mass of whitewater.

The river then mellows somewhat into its most constant, runnable whitewater, including Three Tiers, Trojans and Pig's Trough, named for a side creek where convicts bathed while serving on logging crews. Just downstream is Rock Island Bend, a myrtle-covered island that divides the river in two, just as a photo of it divided the country in two and sparked the river's conservation movement.

While the gradient eases, you still have to get through Newland Cascades, the river's longest rapid, and Big Falls, responsible for several deaths. Only then do you dump out into the Gordon, from where it's a three-hour flatwater paddle to the take-out at Sir John Falls.

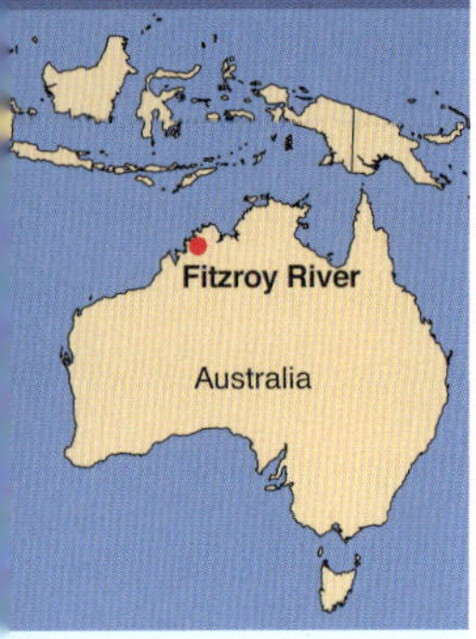


**Experience**
Expert
Anyone can paddle a packraft but you want to be savvy about tropical outback bush camping

**Getting there**
Fitzroy Crossing is 1,500 road miles (2,414km) north of Perth and 250 miles (400km) east of Broome where you can charter a small plane to fly you into the Kimberley. You also needed permission to cross Fossil Downs station land and to paddle through Geicke Gorge NP

**In this location**
Several big rivers radiate from the Kimberley hills. We deliberately chose a straightforward stage in the dry season. Huge tides, sharks, saltwater crocs and near-total inaccessibility make paddling an inflatable to the Timor Sea only for the brave, but you could organise a floatplane pick-up

**On land**
Extended, unsupported land travel is hot, slow and hard. Most enjoy a few days in a rented 4x4 exploring the gorges, pools and upmarket bush camps strung along the 410-mile (600km) Gibb River Road which cuts across the plateau

# FITZROY RIVER, AUSTRALIA

## Packrafting across Australia's remote north-western frontier

A few minutes after the Cessna took off from Fitzroy Crossing, Jeff and I gave each other a thumbs-up. Below us, the Fitzroy River meandered unbroken, northwards into the King Leopold Ranges. The previous Wet had been an unprecedented deluge and now, six months later, there was way more water than we'd hoped.

We were flying into the Kimberley, north-west Australia's rugged, tropical frontier of parched tablelands, seasonal rivers and marginal cattle stations. Whenever a monsoon or cyclone rolled in off the Timor Sea, the languid Fitzroy rose 30 feet (9km) and spread out for miles across its floodplain, cutting off the isolated townships for days.

Dropped off at a bushland airstrip 80 miles (130km) upstream, we were carrying everything we needed for a week: packboats and dried food in hikeable backpacks with footwear to match. The river would transport and sustain us, but we'd still need to tow through shallows or portage over rock bars and log jams.

It was the sort of wilderness adventure that's only possible in a six pound (2.5kg) packraft; a boat that can be rolled up and carried as easily as it's paddled. With temperatures way over 30°C (86°F) and 90 percent humidity, our boats were the amphibious 'mules' which would make it all possible.

I was in the real thing – a taut and durable $900 Alpacka. Jeff chose an inexpensive vinyl pool toy. It floated just the same, but the flaccid hull made paddling excruciating into the first day's headwinds.

On the water by dawn next day, mid-morning saw us at Dimond Gorge, where the Fitzroy parted the Leopold ranges. Ahead of us lay cattle country where the river lost its depth as it meandered south-west. Sure enough, the flow soon dissipated into a jumble of huge boulders, a portage which left me croaking with thirst.

We fully expected the cattle plains to be a tough, fly-ridden trek menaced by feral 'cleanskins'. It turned out to be the highlight. Periodically the river's main channel became choked with flood-borne sand, diverting the flow into the tree-lined banks. Here, under a cool canopy of river gums replete with twittering birds, we'd wade for hours, towing our rafts like polar sleds. Occasionally we squeezed under a log jam, or sank to our knees in quicksands. And most days Jeff would stoically repair his pool toy, punctured by the bluntest twig. Come the evening, we'd spread out across a sandbank with firewood in arm's reach, and recover from the day's efforts.

Following a marathon 20-miler (32km) in 40°C (104°F) heat, the sixth dawn saw us paddle silently past gangly jabiru storks. Sunburnt and exhausted again, we reached the highway bridge a few hours later. Jeff gifted his patched-up pool toy to some frolicking Aboriginal kids while I devised my next Alpacka adventure. We shouldered our lightened packs and headed for the roadhouse for a big drink and a bigger feed.

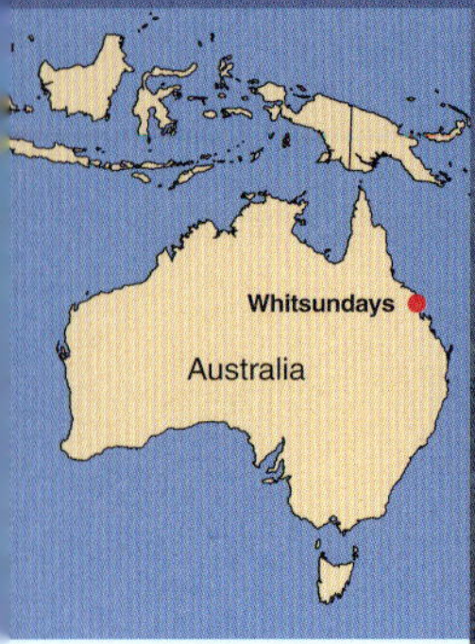


**Experience**
Novice

**Getting there**
There are two major domestic airports situated close to Airlie Beach: Great Barrier Reef Airport on Hamilton Island and Whitsunday Coast Airport 12 miles (19km) inland. You can get to either from Sydney or Brisbane

**In this location**
Save enough time to give the Great Barrier Reef its due, whether by paddle, sailboat or scuba gear. One of the seven wonders of the world, it's made up of more than 2,800 individual coral reefs and stretches 1,300 miles (2,092km) along Australia's north-east coast and is the largest natural feature on earth (it can be seen from outer space)

**On land**
Save some energy to get out of your boats at South Molle Island and hike up Mount Jeffries for spectacular views of the entire Whitsundays' archipelago

# WHITSUNDAY ISLANDS, AUSTRALIA

## A stunning place to waltz with Matilda

Dropping a rudder Down Under doesn't get any better than the Whitsundays, located along Australia's Queensland coast between Mackay and Townsville along the Great Barrier Reef. The region is made up of more than 75 islands strewn about some of the clearest water in the world, each boasting snow-white sandy beaches and vibrant coral reefs.

With more than 70 percent of the area nationally protected, the sheltered islands are bordered by the mountains of the Conway National Park on one side and the Great Barrier Reef on the other, providing miles of tranquil waters for paddling. The national park protection also ensures an abundance of wildlife. As well as the typical wealth of tropical fish you'd expect of a trip to the Great Barrier Reef, you're likely to encounter everything from wallabies and goanna monitor lizards on land, to giant sea turtles, manta rays, dolphins and humpback whales in the water, the latter journeying up from Antarctica to calve (best viewing time: June through to September).

Most kayakers base out of the quaint resort town of Airlie Beach about 70 miles (112km) north of Mackay on a peninsula jutting out into Whitsunday Passage. You can stay in anything from backpacker-style hostels to five-star resorts, and everything in between as you plan your trip.

Provisions and gear ready, you can then water taxi to five-mile-long (8km) Whitehaven Beach on the south-east side of Whitsunday Island, considered one of the most beautiful beaches in the world. Here you camp, snorkel and take a day trip to nearby Haselwood Island (or hike over to Chance Bay).

From here options abound: you can paddle north along the island's east coast with the wind, hiking for spectacular views on the hills of Hill Inlet along the way, to Peter Bay and Crayfish Beach in Mackeral Bay on Hook Island, known for its great camping. Longer trips can also be taken to Maureens Cove, Steens Beach, Hayman Island and Black Island, all offering pristine snorkelling and swimming every stroke of the way.

That said, there are a few essentials to pack for any sea kayak trip in the region. Foremost is sunscreen and a wide-brimmed sunhat – the south's thin ozone layer easily causes sunburn – as well as plenty of water to ward off the dehydration that comes with paddling Down Under. And make sure you have a good set of snorkelling gear. You won't find better water for it anywhere on the planet, and not doing so is as much of a sacrilege as forsaking Vegemite, meat pies and Fosters.

**Experience**
Novice

**Getting there**
It's out of the way, but most airlines fly there. Hint: since you're in the neighbourhood anyway, consider extending your stay with a quick visit to New Zealand

**In this location**
Believe it or not, Fiji also has whitewater. Try a trip on the Upper Navua and Wainikoroiluva (Luva) Rivers on Viti Levu

**On land**
Get your shopping (and bargaining) fix at Suva Municipal Market on the main island of Viti Levu ... it's the largest and most lively market in Fiji

# FIJI

## Drink deep from this cocktail of island delights

When Captain Bligh floated by the Fiji islands after being set adrift by the crew of *The Bounty* in 1789, little did he realise that the cannibal-infested islands would soon become a Mecca for sea kayaking.

First spotted by Dutchman Abel Tasman in 1643, with Captain Cook sighting them again in 1774, more than 97 percent of Fiji's 275,000 square miles (709,000km$^2$) is water, meaning plenty of exploration room for paddlers. As well as being home to more than 300 islands – only 100 of which are inhabited – the country is also located in nutrient-rich currents, spelling fish-laden waters for fishing and diving.

One of more popular archipelagos to kayak is the Kadavu group, a cluster of volcanic masses about 60 miles (97km) south of the main island of Viti Levu. Lagoons, passages and remote beaches are sheltered from the South Pacific swells by one of the world's largest coral formations. Within the chain are the islands of Ono, Dravuni, Buliya and Kadavu. You can paddle resort to resort, staying in thatch-roofed cabanas, island to island and beach to beach.

The main logistical hurdle to work through is getting permission to camp (check with local outfitters for proper protocol). Although less than 17 percent of Fijian land is privately owned – the rest is either owned by native tribes or was transferred to the government when Fiji gained its freedom in 1970 after 96 years of British rule – you'll need approval to paddle, which often requires a bit more than a handshake.

Expect to take part in several sevusevu ceremonies along the way, all of which revolve around kava, a local drink made from the pulverised root of the narcotic Yaqona plant. Served from a large wooden bowl, the drink has been used throughout Fiji's history for everything from consummating business deals to welcoming visitors. When it comes to sea kayaking, you'll partake in it to land on beaches, paddle local waters and camp. And while the buzz that comes with the pepper-based concoction is diluted from the early days (some sailors reported temporary paralysis), expect to feel a little something from the stimulant; local healers still use it to treat everything from tooth decay to gonorrhea.

Permission granted, don't be surprised if your host drapes fresh leis around your necks, lets you overnight in a romantic thatched-roof hut, and even buries a pig wrapped in banana leaves to roast in your honour. All this from sipping a narcotic cocktail with a village chief whose ancestors used to be cannibals.

And bring a fishing rod. Midstream in the Equatorial current, which flows east from the trenches of Peru, Fiji's waters are rich in nutrients, meaning they're also teeming with fish – which is perfect for snorkelling and supper. And it's certainly a better alternative than what the natives ate in Captain Bligh's day.

**Experience**
Intermediate – Expert

**Getting there**
Fly into Kauai's Lihue airport and drive to the end of Highway 560 on Kauai's north-west shore to Haena and Ke'e Beach

**In this location**
For an easy river trip (perfect for stand up paddleboards even), float the Hanalei River into Hanalei Bay

**On land**
Hike the 11-mile (18km) Kalalau Trail from Ke'e Beach to Kalalau Valley. The most popular section is from Ke'e to the lush valley of HanakāpīAi. You can also hike an 8-mile (13km) round trip to a waterfall or 4-mile (6km) round trip to HanakāpīAi Beach. Hiking beyond HanakapiAi requires a state permit

# HAWAI'I

## Touring a tropical paradise

Once used as a trade route by ancient islanders, Hawai'i's rugged Na Pali Coast, located on the north coast of Kauai, lets experienced sea kayakers follow the natives' wakes in a watery wonderland. The stretch serves up golden, sandy beaches, towering coastal cliffs, ancient ruins, pristine snorkelling and at-a-glance beachcombing.

In short, the north coast of Kauai is the quintessential Hawaiian kayak trip, packed with the scenery that has made the islands famous. And there is no better way to see it all than from a sea kayak, which lets you paddle through sea caves and stop to snorkel, beachcomb and revel in waterfalls on the Garden Isle along the way.

The waterfalls owe themselves to some of the most concentrated rainfall on the planet, combined with cliffs towering 3,000 feet (914m) up from the shore. It's these same cliffs that make the region so isolated. This 15-mile (24km) stretch of coastline literally means 'the Cliffs', with most of it inaccessible due to the sheer faces plunging straight down thousands of feet into the sea. The only way to see them is by foot, via the 11-mile (18km) Kalalau Trail (see sidebar), or by boat.

While sightseeing boats tote tourists along the coast, a sea kayak (usually a sit-on-top) provides a more up close and personal view. The most popular stretch to paddle runs 17 miles (27km) from Ke'e Beach to Polihale State Park, with most people electing to camp at least a night or two along the way. You will have to purchase camping permits to stop and camp at Kalalau and Miloli'i Beach 15 May – 17 September; no other private boat landings are allowed. Ambitious day trippers can make it to Kalalau Beach and back, a total of 22 miles (35km), but leave early and monitor the winds.

En route you'll also pass by the ancient Hawai'ian fishing village of Nu'alolo Kai, but you'll have to take it in from the water; private boaters aren't allowed to land. You'll see plenty of fish, however, as well as dolphins and whales, and even more if you bring your snorkel. Kauai offers the oldest and most protected reef ecosystem of all the major Hawai'ian islands, with a third of its fish found nowhere else in the world. You'll likely also see the ancient Honu (Hawai'ian green sea turtle) that graze on the limu (algae) growing on the local reefs.

The only other thing to remember is safety. Na Pali's remote location makes help and rescue challenging. In particular, pay special attention to and get local information on the area's currents, swells and shore breaks (Hanakapi'ai Beach has especially hazardous conditions). Stick to the summer months for your planning; they're the best for sea kayaking due to calmer swell.

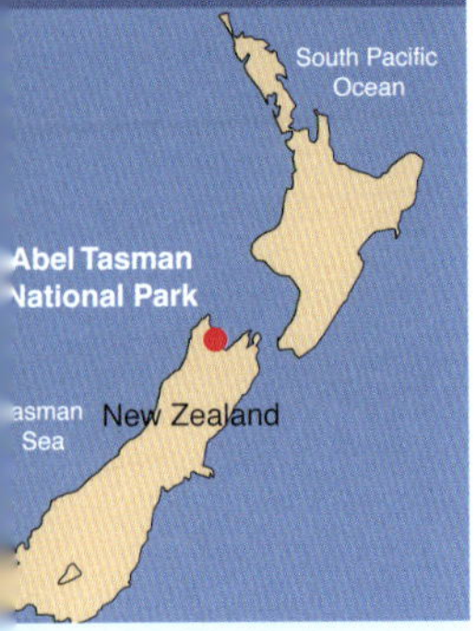


**Experience**
Novice

**Getting there**
Fly from Wellington, Christchurch or Auckland to Takara Airport in Nelson. There are regular and on-demand bus services to the park from Nelson and other local towns as well as water taxi services

**In this location**
The Shotover River in the outdoor Mecca of Queenstown offers thrills and spills New Zealand-style

**On land**
The park is also one of New Zealand's best walks; if you can't paddle the whole thing, hike its main trail. The track is suitable for all ages and can be hiked in 3-5 days

# ABEL TASMAN NATIONAL PARK, NEW ZEALAND

## Hut-to-hut kayaking in the land of the Southern Cross

Little did Dutchman Abel Tasman realise when he spotted New Zealand some 370 years ago that the South Island's best kayaking hotspot would soon be named after him. Located at the north end of the South Island, Abel Tasman National Park boasts more than 58 square miles ($150km^2$) and 31 miles (50km) of shoreline to explore by paddlecraft, with sandy beaches for those wishing to camp beneath the Southern Cross and huts for those who prefer shelter.

Established in 1942, the park is New Zealand's smallest, stretching from Wainui Inlet in Golden Bay on its northern reaches to Marahau in the south. But its vistas and reputation among kayakers are grand. Renowned for its temperate climate perfect for paddling, the Abel Tasman coastal track is listed as one of New Zealand's great walks. But it's every bit as good when you see it from the water.

On a typical day's paddle you'll explore coves, lagoons and estuaries. You'll also encounter freshwater rivers, bay crossings, offshore islands, sculpted rocks and vast stretches of golden, sand beaches that owe their beauty to millions of polished quartz crystals from the area's granite. Further inshore are manuka and kanuka forests, as well as nikau palm. Here you'll see a dynamic cross section of New Zealand's bird life, from bellbird and kereru to pukeko, herons and oystercatchers in the estuaries. Turn your eyes seaward and you'll discover a world of marine life, including penguins, seals and dolphins.

It's also a good place to polish up on your local history, from the area's early Maori occupation to later European settlement (largely thanks to Mr Tasman). Throughout your paddle you'll also pass several archaeological sites to explore.

But as alluring as all of these features are, perhaps the park's main appeal for paddlers is its overnight options. The park's coastal trail is managed by the Department of Conservation and is open year-round. Along its route there are huts, campsites and lodges to stay in including Totaranui, a campground. Booking is essential. Reserve a spot in a hut and you can leave your tent and stove at home, and share stories with other like-minded travellers. Camp at one of its designated beach sites and you can sip a glass of New Zealand chardonnay under the Southern Cross.

Because it's a national park, there are regulations to follow. You can only have campfires in designated fireplaces and you have to take out all of your trash. It's also advisable to treat all your drinking water unless it comes from a certified tap.

Mosquitoes and sand flies are the only real potential annoyances. But don't let them get to you; it's a small price to pay for paddling in paradise.

**Experience**
Intermediate – Expert

**Getting there**
From Auckland, either take the ferry or water taxi, or fly to the island's Claris Airport. In peak season, be sure to book transport well in advance

**In this location**
If you have a few days to spare, the Auckland area offers great touring as well, including such hotspots as the Bay of Islands, Whangaruru, Whananaki and Ngunguru. If you don't want to bring your own boat, you can rent singles and tandems from various hire shops on the island

**On land**
The island is a haven for the New Zealand pastime of tramping. The Department of Conservation has created more than 60 miles (97km) of walking tracks throughout the island, including the popular Over the Top trail up Mt Hobson, which takes about six hours. The island also boasts several natural hot springs to soak paddle-weary shoulders

# GREAT BARRIER ISLAND, NEW ZEALAND

## A wildlife wonderland for sea kayakers

Named by Captain James Cook for the formidable barrier it creates between the Pacific Ocean and Hauraki Gulf, New Zealand's Great Barrier Island, located about 60 miles (97km) north-east of Auckland, is a kayakers' paradise. With an area of 110 square miles (285km$^2$), it's the country's fourth-largest island, whose highest point, Mount Hobson, rises over 2,000 feet (610m) above the sea.

It's this water environment that entices kayakers over from the mainland. The island has contrasting coastal environments; while its Pacific-ravaged eastern coast comprises long beaches, dunes and crashing surf, its western coast is sheltered and calm, harbouring countless secluded bays, coves and inlets. That's the place to head for to sample some of the country's best sea kayaking.

While the island is inhabited by under 1,000 people, most of whom live in the main harbour towns of

Whangaparaparapara, Tryphena, Port FitzRoy and Okupu, it also offers great southern solitude. More than 60 percent of the island is administered by the Department of Conservation (DOC) as a nature reserve. This means you'll see everything from tracks of regenerating kanuka bush and new-growth forests of kauri trees, once a staple for loggers, as well as such bird life as brown teal ducks, black petrel seabirds and North Island Kaka parrots. Keep your eyes peeled around you on the water as well, as you'll likely also paddle with dolphins and sight whales.

Many paddlers start at the ferry harbours of Tryphena, where a four-hour paddle leads you to campgrounds at Whangaparapara, and another four hours on, at Port Fitzroy. Located right on the water's edge and perfect for paddlers, the campgrounds are maintained by the DOC. The only real regulation is that no fires are allowed, so make sure to pack a stove in your kit. You can also stretch your legs and walk a half hour to stores from each campsite if you're in need of libations or provisions. It's worth taking a night paddle under the southern stars to churn up iridescent phosphorescence with every stroke.

Another popular spot for paddlers is the northern end of Kaitoke Beach and the Kaitoke Swamp, which offers calmer paddling than the open ocean. If you find yourself near the north end of the island, you can also polish up on your shipwreck history. Just offshore is the site of one of New Zealand's worst shipwrecks in the sinking of the *SS Wairapa* on 29 October 1894, in which 121 lives were lost. Two grave sites can be found on the island's northernmost beach.

# SOUTH ISLAND, NEW ZEALAND

## Access all areas – in a helicopter

The west coast of New Zealand's South Island around the town of Greymouth is a very special place for whitewater kayakers; it is one of the only places in the world where kayakers can call up the local helicopter pilot and book a shuttle ride up into the Southern Alps. It is just as easy as calling a cab, simply phone up and request a lift up to the put-in of your chosen run. One of the most experienced helicopter pilots on the west coast is Bruce Dando, he is an old kayaker and knows every river and put-in like the back of his hand.

Every heli-kayaking day is special, waking up knowing that today is the day, rushing breakfast and jumping into the car, racing to the meeting point, anxious not to miss the slot and then waiting, because you are early, or Bruce is late! Then you hear the sound of the small helicopter's rotors chopping through the air, getting gradually louder and louder, everybody scanning the sky for the chopper, 'There he is!' shouts someone pointing up into the sky.

Time is money and the aim of the game is to get the first two kayaks loaded onto the helicopter as quick as possible, then up into the air you go, crammed into the small bubble cockpit. Looking down at the river from the cockpit allows you a fleeting glimpse at the rapids that will confront you on your day's whitewater adventure; be aware that rapids that look big from a helicopter are really big when you are on the water.

After no time at all the helicopter has landed in the middle of nowhere, you jump out, untie your kayak and paddle from the skids and whoosh! The helicopter is gone, you are left alone far, far away from road or civilisation, just you and your team, your kayaks and the river, let the adventure begin. There are many rivers on New Zealand's west coast that are best accessed by helicopter: the Hokitika, the Arahura, the Perth and the Whitcombe are all classics.

**Grade**
3-5

**Experience**
Intermediate – Expert

**Getting there**
Fly to New Zealand and drive to Greymouth on South Island (there is a ferry service from North Island). Stay at Lake Mahinapua Campsite where there are often other paddlers staying too

**In this location**
There are many rivers that do not need helicopter access that can be enjoyed on the west coast. Try the Kakopotahi or the Styx if you want to enjoy a hike up the river before you paddle back down it

**On land**
The west coast of New Zealand provides plenty of entertainment opportunities for those who love playing outside, instead of heli-kayaking try heli-hiking or heli-fishing!

MX
adidas

**Experience**
Novice

**Getting there**
There are lots of clubs all around the world; Australia and Hawai'i have the most, check the internet for details of the closest club to you

**In this location**
Varies depending on location

**On land**
Varies depending on location

# SOUTH-EAST PACIFIC

## Timless adventure – outrigger canoes have a great past and a bight future

Originating from south-east Asia, Pacific outrigger canoes were used to transport people and trading goods from island to island. Today outrigger canoes are raced in both sprint and marathon events and also used for recreational paddling.

Outrigger canoes were developed by paddlers wishing to undertake journeys across the ocean; aware that a single hulled dug-out canoe was too unstable to safely ride through the swell and waves, an outrigger was added to the dug-out canoe to increase stability. Smaller outrigger canoes normally have just one outrigger that is fixed to the left side of the hull, larger canoes often feature an outrigger on both sides.

Besides recreational paddling there are several competitive disciplines for outrigger canoe paddlers to take part in; canoe surfing and sprint and marathon races. Racers can choose a one person OC1 canoe or be part of a team or two, three, four, six or 12 paddlers. Sprint races take place on short courses between 820 feet (250m) and 1,640 feet (500m) and longer marathon events often take place in the open sea. It is then the responsibility of the steersman to keep the canoe on track and the crew safe. There are also longer events in the six person, OC6, class, a support boat carries three extra crew members, periodically a relief crew member is dropped into the sea in front of the canoe, as the canoe paddles past the new crew member climbs in on the outrigger side and the other paddler rolls out and is collected by the support boat. The rolling crew changes require incredible judgement on behalf of the steersman as he or she must steer the canoe close enough to the paddler in the water so that the crew can climb in without being run down and without the canoe losing any speed.

Outrigger canoe surfing is one of the most amazing ocean sports, the sight of an outrigger canoe carving across the face of a huge ocean wave is incredible; each member of the team must work harmoniously together to ensure that the canoe is not engulfed by the breaking wave. The steersman uses their paddle to control the direction of the canoe on the wave, the middle crew members lean into the wave to prevent the canoe from capsizing and the front paddler provides extra paddle strokes to keep the canoe surfing on the face of the wave. Most outrigger surfing events take place in Hawai'i in huge surf with OC4 or OC6 canoes.

Outrigger canoeing has a rich history that dates back thousands of years and is an important part of history and heritage for many Pacific islanders. Today it still plays an important part of everyday life for many people of all ages who live by the ocean.

**Experience**
Intermediate

**Getting there**
Bowron Lake Provincial Park is located in the Cariboo Mountains in central British Columbia, and Wells on Highway 26 is the nearest community. International visitors can fly in to Calgary or Vancouver. Then you can catch either a train or internal flight to Quensel. From here it is 75 miles (120km) to the park

**In this location**
If 10 days on the circuit isn't enough for you then there's so much to explore and discover that you can do any number of day or overnight trips on the Park's waters

**On land**
Swimming, hiking in nearby mountains or fishing for bull, rainbow and lake trout and the famous kokanee salmon. A visit to the historic town of Barkerville is also well worth doing if you have the time

# BOWRON LAKE NATIONAL PARK, CANADA

## Following the call of the loon

The Bowron Lake National Park is a large wilderness area situated on the western slopes of the Cariboo Mountain Range and is home to the world-renowned Bowron Lake Circuit. In 1926, thanks to the work done by Frank Kibbee and Thomas and Eleanor McCabe, the British Columbia provincial government classified this area as a game reserve. In 1961 it was reclassified as a park and named after John Bowron, a gold rush pioneer who became the Gold Commissioner at Barkerville, now a famous restored gold rush town of the 1860s.

The park is a beautiful region of mountains, lakes and rivers. And the canoe circuit is formed by an amazing series of geological faults, which have combined to create a 72-mile (116km) rectangular circuit of lakes and rivers, connected by portage trails. All nestled between pristine Canadian wilderness and overlooked by breathtaking snow-covered peaks. The park circuit can be paddled from May through to October and a typical trip takes between seven and ten days. Highlights include: Wolverine Bay, Lake Isaac, the Cariboo River, Sandy Lake, Spectacle Lake and Bowron Lake. You can bring in your own canoe and gear or there are several outfitters in the area that can provide you with everything that you will need for a successful trip, including a portage trolley for transporting your laden canoe over the six miles (10km) of portage trails along the way.

Being in a National Park means that there is some red tape to get through before you head out into the wild, including having your loaded canoe weighed by the Park Rangers. There is a limit on how much you can carry in the boat while portaging (60lbs / 27kg) and anything over this must be carried on your back. This is to help keep the portage trails in good order. Once you've got your permit, loaded your kit and completed the checks, it's out onto the water. Despite the large numbers of people completing the circuit each year its vast area means that you'll be enjoying peace and solitude almost from the off.

With a fully laden canoe the first portage-filled day will be tough, but as the miles go by, so you will settle into a routine and the cares and worries of everyday life will fall away as you become one with the rhythms of nature. Rise, breakfast, load, paddle, portage, load, paddle, dinner cooked on a crackling campfire followed by contented sleep under a canopy of stars.

Wildlife is all around you on the Bowron Circuit and it's common to see bear (black and grizzly), osprey, moose, beaver, caribou and otters. And as you settle down for your first night's sleep, in one of the well-appointed campsites, the haunting call of the Loons ringing out across the silent water will leave you in no doubt that the Bowron Lakes Circuit is a never-to-be-forgotten paddle on the wild side.

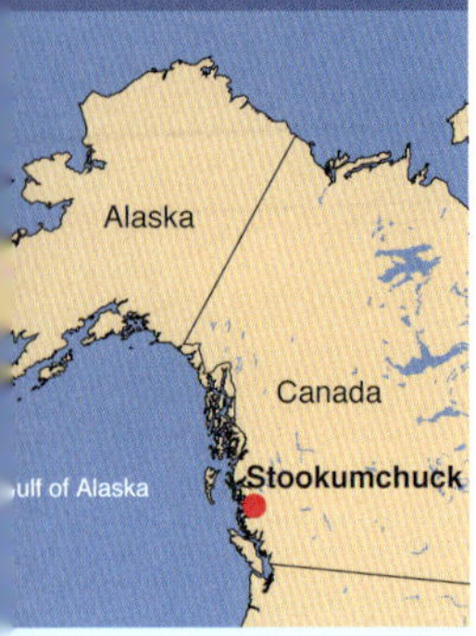


**Experience**
Expert

**Getting there**
From central Vancouver, drive 25 minutes to Horseshoe Bay Ferry Terminal and take the ferry to Langdale. Then drive an hour and a half to Egmont, where you can paddle or hike to Skook from the marina

**In this location**
Since you have your whitewater boats (hopefully also creekers), take time after the ferry back to venture up toward Squamish and Whistler, where you can paddle such classics as Tatlow Creek, and the Elaho, Callaghan and Cheakamus rivers

**On land**
The hike to the rapids is beautiful, especially with the stop at Brown Lake. To simply relax and watch the phenomena, stop at the overlook at Roland Point

# SKOOKUMCHUCK NARROWS, BRITISH COLUMBIA, CANADA

## Tidal rapids that lure kayakers from all over the world

Epic kayak surf isn't just restricted to rivers or shore breaks. A tidal rapid in British Columbia lures paddlers from the world over to an almost surreal glassy wave that serves up some of the best surf on the continent.

The rapid's name is Skookumchuck, a Chinook name for 'Strong Water'. It's aptly named. It is located in Skookumchuck Narrows Provincial Park and the ocean-water rapid forms when nearly 32 billion cubic feet (a billion $m^3$) of water from the incoming tide accelerates through a tight channel connecting Sechelt and Jervis inlets. At peak flows, it forms the fastest and largest salt water rapids in North America, whose current reaches speeds of up to 17 knots (32kph), creating a colossal kayaking monster.

Of course, paying attention to the tide chart is paramount: you want to time your trip so you're there when the rapid is forming. This means arriving when it's on the way up, which happens twice daily, and leaving on the ebb. Pick up a chart and look for the maximum flood (the fastest speed that particular tide will run), and then look for the ebb and slack. The best surfing, for both new-school freestyle moves and full-on glassy carving, occurs when the tide is running between 12-14 knots (22-26kph). Also pay attention to the timing; the flow usually begins about two hours before max flood and lasts until two hours after. That means you have about a four-hour surf window in which to do everything from phonics monkeys to window shades, and everything in between. And beware the dark; many a paddler has enjoyed a sunset surf session only to paddle out in the dark.

Time it right, however, and you're in for an experience like no other. At first you'll wonder why the fuss (and headache to get there). But then the current will start flowing and a small ripple will form. Then it'll get bigger and bigger, and eventually start breaking. Right around then you'll realise, 'Oh my God, this thing looks awesome!' and then it'll get bigger still, until it's a frothing monster testing the sport's best. The foam pile stays massive for hours, with the wave re-forming even when the tide starts slowing down. Just be aware the whirlpool in the eddy downstream eats unsuspecting kayakers alive.

The only other real drawback is getting there: to experience nature's power in such a raw form requires a trip to the boondocks. You need to get to British Columbia, then catch a ferry, then drive, and then either paddle or carry your kayak a mile and a half (2.4km) to the tidal spot (more than 50,000 people hike there per year).

Then, once the tide has run its course, it's an equal hassle to get back. You can either paddle back to the town of Egmont, which requires paddling against the tide after your muscles are already worn, or you can hike out, which means shouldering your boat for 45 minutes. The good news: you can wash off the salt with a dip in freshwater Brown Lake.

WERNER

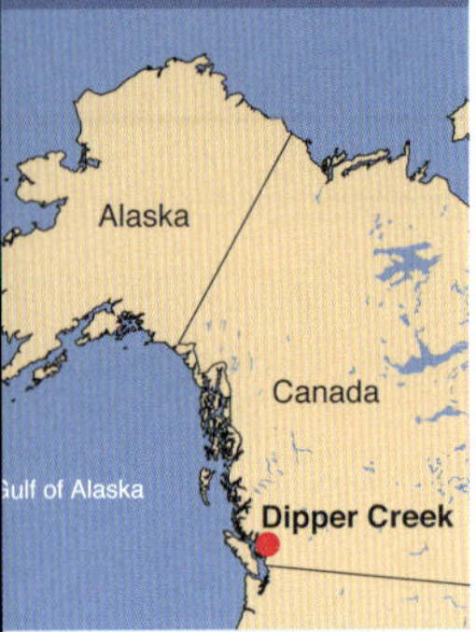


**Grade**
5-6

**Experience**
Expert

**Getting there**
Dipper Creek is in the Squamish area of British Columbia, Canada. A long hike through dense forest will get you to the edge of the canyon for your first look at this unbelievable creek

**In this location**
BC is full of amazing rivers and creeks: the Ashlu, Elaho, Squamish and the Tatlow, there are more opportunities to paddle whitewater in BC than there is time

**On land**
A serious attempt at Dipper Creek will need land support, a few guys with long ropes and climbing gear to help if anybody or the whole team needs to exit the canyon. After Dipper Creek the only thing you will need is a cold beer and rest

# DIPPER CREEK, BRITISH COLUMBIA, CANADA

## A world of waterfalls

Dipper Creek is a test; it requires expert skills, stamina, good judgement and guts. It was first attempted by The Range Life crew in 2008 after a long phase of scouting and preparation. The creek itself is deep inside a narrow canyon in the forests of British Columbia, many of the waterfalls and rapids are very difficult to inspect from the river and the chance of trees falling into the canyon, causing a potentially deadly hazard, increases the risk and challenge for those brave and skilled enough to attempt this run.

Depending where you put in there is a good chance to warm up on boulder parcours and a few smaller waterfalls before a side creek joins and the fun really begins. A series of bigger waterfalls one after another will challenge the team: first up is Double Dip, jump down the first drop into a small pool, quickly orientate yourself and set up for the second drop. Next up comes the famous Big Dipper, a huge 65-foot (20m) sliding waterfall, as you accelerate down the slide your pulse is racing as fast as your kayak. Before reaching the bottom you must tuck your head down in front of you to minimise the impact on your upper body and face as you land in the pool at the bottom, holding your paddle hard against the side of your kayak and taking a last look at the landing zone before you tuck up and take the force of the impact. Boom! Then roll up. Yes! Success.

In the second half of Dipper Creek is Vertigo Canyon, the entry drop is a complex line over a twisting waterfall that lands in pulsating unpredictable water that pushes into the canyon wall. The landing is difficult to escape from and just after the first drop two easier waterfalls follow, the second landing is into a beautiful pool of still water deep down inside the canyon. The feelings of intensity, of loneliness, in the canyon are overwhelmed by the concentration required to safely navigate such challenging whitewater. It's all about you, your kayak and the water. Dipper Creek is special, it requires the combination of so many whitewater skills. It is like no other river in the world.

SURF KAYAKING

**Grade**
3-4

**Experience**
Intermediate - Expert

**Getting there**
Travelling to Montreal is the easiest part of the journey; finding and paddling out the waves in the Lachine rapids is very tricky. The river is very wide and fast flowing, it is best to follow a local paddler if you have never been before

**In this location**
The state of Quebec is one of the best paddling destinations in the world, there is whitewater to suit all abilities and tastes

**On land**
Montreal is a fascinating city with a rich cultural history and many festivals throughout the year, getting bored is not an option

# LACHINE RAPIDS, MONTREAL, CANADA

## Surfing huge waves through the middle of a city

The big standing waves formed on the Saint Lawrence river in Montreal in Quebec, Canada, are some of the most famous river waves in the world for kayakers, surfers and stand up paddle boarders. There are many different waves to choose from, each running at its best depending on the water level; the most famous wave is Big Joe which reaches a height of over 6 feet (2m) at optimum water levels, others are called Pyramid, Kong and Maverick.

Surfing waves in a kayak at Lachine is a unique experience, paddling out into the middle of the river to find the green monsters is an adventure in itself, comparable with a journey over the ocean in a tiny plastic freestyle kayak battling powerful currents and swirling whirlpools. Once you make it out to the wave the real fun starts, Lachine waves are big, steep and fast. Surfing around and bouncing up into the air you feel almost out of control. Surf up to the peak of the wave and line up for your move, angle the kayak, make your last power stroke and shoot down the wave, catch the bounce at the bottom and you are airborne! Quick as a flash, turn your body through the pre-rehearsed movements of your planned move and then you are back surfing and bouncing on the face of the wave. There is no time to rest on these waves, an athletic paddling style is needed to maintain the surf, and fitness and strength are necessary to perform multiple moves ride after ride.

Surfing the waves is the aim of the game, but sitting in the line-up watching others perform their tricks is also an enjoyable part of the Lachine experience, watching some of the best freestyle kayakers in the world bouncing their kayaks up into the air and rotating into combinations of moves that seem almost impossible; the secret is to accelerate down the face of the wave as fast as possible and use this speed to launch into the air in front of the wave. Boom! Another huge airborne trick and the tired kayaker falls off the back of the wave. You are up again, surf out onto the wave, get settled and set up, then you are back in the zone. Nothing else in the world matters now just you, your kayak and the wave, which trick to hit next and how to land it back on the wave: this is life at its best.

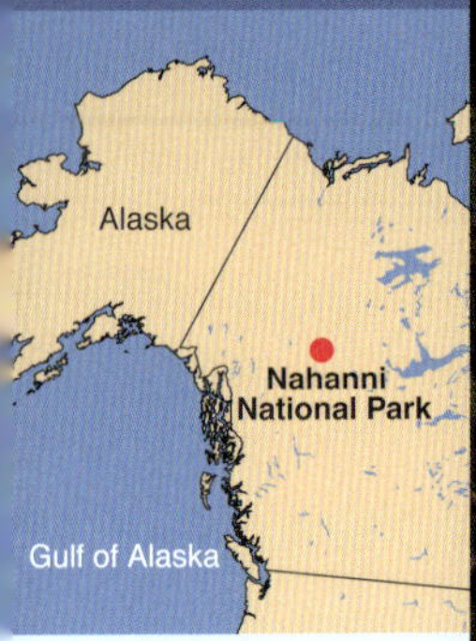


**Grade**
1-4

**Experience**
Intermediate – Expert

**Getting there**
There's a price to pay for such wilderness; it's in the boonies. There are daily direct flights to Fort Simpson from Yellowknife. Alternatively, Fort Simpson can also be reached via a scenic drive from Fort Nelson, British Columbia on the Liard Trail Highway (watch out for bison!), or a drive from High Level, Alberta, skirting the Mackenzie River. With no public roads in the park itself, most paddlers access it via chartered floatplane from Fort Simpson

**In this location**
The Flat River offers a great Class 3-5 section within Nahanni National Park. Most people access it from Seaplane Lake, and take four to five days to float it to its confluence with the South Nahanni

**On land**
Pack light for portaging Virginia Falls, but bring a pair of solid hiking shoes. The area offers spectacular side hikes in the Ragged Range, including the renowned Cirque of the Unclimbables

# NAHANNI NATIONAL PARK, CANADA

## One of the most spectacular destinations on earth

For a true dose of Jack London's north country wilderness from a canoe, it doesn't get any better than the South Nahanni River in Canada's Northwest Territories. Navigable from June to September, the Nahanni's big volume and powerful currents command respect – the stretch should only be run by experienced canoeists with well-practised rescue skills – but its rewards come on many levels, foremost are its wilderness and scenery.

The Nahanni is one of the most spectacular destinations on Earth, with a backdrop of towering granite monoliths that will make your jaw drop (the area is as popular with climbers as it is with paddlers for its massive multi-pitch walls). Reservations are required for all river trips in the park, with the park service recommending getting them well in advance due to demand. To help ensure safety, parties also have to register at park headquarters beforehand and upon return.

Do so and you're in for a true treat. The park offers six different river sections to paddle, all varying in difficulty and all with inspiring vistas every stroke of the way. Most paddlers tackling the South Nahanni proper begin at one of the two put-ins – Virginia Falls (7 to 10 days) or Rabbitkettle Lake (10-14 days).

In the 73 miles (118km) from Rabbitkettle to Virginia Falls, the river meanders through a broad valley, with no major rapids of consequence. All that changes at Virginia Falls, one of the most spectacular waterfalls on the planet (and an obvious portage), measuring twice the height of Niagara Falls. Below the torrent, the river enters the first of four massive canyons. First is a 91-mile (147km) section down to Kraus Hot Springs, with up to Class 3 rapids including Canyon, Figure 8 and George's Riffle (most parties bring spray decks for this section).

A 22-mile (35km) flatwater section called the Splits, where the river branches into several different channels, takes you to the park boundary. After another 19 miles (30km) you'll arrive at the confluence of the Liard River at Nahanni Butte, where you can continue on to its joining with the MacKenzie River at Fort Simpson.

Several shorter paddling options also exist, most above Rabbitkettle Lake. For advanced paddlers, Moose Ponds (or Rock Gardens) marks the headwaters of the South Nahanni, offering 31 miles (50km) of continuous Class 2-4 (depending on flow). It usually takes five to seven days to reach Rabbitkettle Lake. An alternate put-in is at Island Lakes halfway down, shortening the trip to three to four days. It's on this stretch that you can hike to Glacier Lake and the magnificent Cirque of the Unclimbables.

Still another option for experienced canoeists is the Little Nahnni, accessible from Tungsten. The 56-mile (90km) trip serves up Class 2-4 rapids before joining the South Nahanni between the Rock Gardens and Island Lakes.

**Grade**
1-3

**Experience**
Intermediate – Expert

**Getting there**
Take a scheduled flight to Norman Wells Airport and then charter a plane to the Mountain River

**In this location**
It's all about the Mountain River here and the trip is long enough to fill a whole visit

**On land**
It's well worth packing a decent pair of trail shoes too as a day or two hiking in the surrounding mountains is highly recommended

# MOUNTAIN RIVER, CANADA

## Multi-day magic on the mountain

The Mountain River rises high in the spires of the Mackenzie Mountains and flows almost 230 miles (370km) until it finally converges with the Mackenzie River. Over its journey the jagged peaks of the mountains fill and dominate the backdrop, as the river weaves its way through craggy ridges, desolate, barren land and a series of breathtaking canyons with sheer vertical walls of rock enclosing the river on both sides.

The Mountain River Valley has no permanent inhabitants so this is a wilderness trip in the true sense of the word and even getting to the start point is an adventure in itself. The journey starts with loading gear, people and canoes into a floatplane for a flight to the scenic Willow Handle Lake. From there it's time to shoulder the kit and boats, and start practising your portage skills, with a short hike to Push Me Pull Me Creek. This is again more portaging than paddling until you finally reach Blackfeather Creek, and blessed deeper water and this in turn then takes you finally on to the grey, silt-laden waters of the Mountain River. It's hard work but the sense of starting right from the source of the river gives a real sense of achievement. The full trip will take between ten and twelve days, depending on the water level of the river, and you may want to take longer to allow for rest days and exploring the surrounding mountain wilderness.

The river moves swiftly throughout its length and you'll encounter many easy rapids and wave trains. In the canyons things get a little more serious, but all the rapids can usually be run and are easy to inspect, portage or line if needed. The whitewater is just enough to keep you focused and the fun factor high, but it never gets so difficult as to take away from the magnificent surroundings and the plethora of wildlife that surrounds you. Indeed you may not see any other people while you're on the Mountain, but you'll be sharing the river environment with caribou, bears, both black and grizzly, wolverines, moose and wolves!

As the days glide past you'll find yourself slipping into an easy, natural rhythm as you become tuned to the nuances of the river as it takes you under its spell. Laying on beaches at night under a blanket of jet punctuated with a million stars, as the sound of the river gently lulls you into restful and worry-free sleep.

Pitching and breaking camp will become second nature and your paddle will feel like an extension of your body as you bob and weave your way down the magical Mountain River, working as one with your canoe partner, in one of the world's last true wilderness terrains.

# ALGONQUIN PROVINCIAL PARK, CANADA

## Classic canoeing in a paddling paradise

**Experience**
Novice

**Getting there**
It's an easy drive from both Toronto and Ottawa. Highway 60 runs through the south of the Park, while the Trans-Canada Highway bypasses it to the north

**In this location**
Just across the provincial border in Quebec, La Vérendrye Wildlife Reserve offers a network of rivers and lakes for canoe-trippers of all levels

**On land**
The Park has 14 interpretive trails, as well as three areas of back country hiking trails. These trails have their own dedicated lakeside campsites. The Visitor Centre contains cultural and natural exhibits, a detailed relief map, theatre, outdoor viewing deck and The Algonquin Room art gallery. It's worth joining the weekly wolf howl programs, held every Thursday in August

Established in 1893, Ontario's Algonquin Provincial Park is the oldest provincial park in Canada. That's not to say canoeists have been going there longer than anywhere else, but it became a park for a reason and that reason involves paddling.

Named a National Historic Site of Canada in 1992, the park has more than 2,400 lakes and 745 miles (1,200km) of streams and rivers, all yours for the taking. Included in this watery web is aptly named Canoe Lake as well as such rivers as the Petawawa, Madawaska, Tim, Magnetawan, Gull, Amable du Fond and Barron. Any one of these waterways would make the region a destination worth visiting in its own right. Lump them all together and you get a canoeing wonderland found nowhere else in the world. Arguably offering some of Canada's best canoeing, its waterways form a whopping 1,242 miles (2,000km) of interconnected paddling routes – plenty of room to get lost should you so desire. Head out for a three-day trip or a three-month trip; the further you go, the more immersed in wilderness you become. And you can rent everything from your canoe to camping gear through one of the park's outfitters, making logistics as easy as your paddle strokes.

And that wilderness is as wild as it gets – even by Canadian standards. The reason is its latitude, located at the border of the coniferous forests to the north and the more deciduous forests to the south. This unique mixture supports a wide array of plant and animal species, offering every bit as much solace as the fur-trading voyageurs of yesteryear experienced. Don't be surprised to see moose, deer, beavers and even bear from the seat of your canoe, and hear the call of loons or even wolves over the crackle of your campfire.

While there are more than 1,200 car-accessible campsites in eight campgrounds along Highway 60 in the south end of the park, and 100 more in the Park's northern and eastern reaches, your best bet to truly experience this wilderness is to head to the Park's 'interior' camping areas, those sites only accessible by foot or boat (all have fire pits and can be reserved through Ontario Parks).

To reach the more remote sites in the Park, expect to partake in the popular Canadian pastime of portaging, which means carrying your gear on your back as well as in your canoe (but still bring the Dutch oven). Thankfully, the Park maintains one of two types of portages between most of the park's lakes – those coloured red on the map are well maintained and well travelled; those marked black are a little more suspect and harder to follow. But you can take solace in the fact that, as Canada's oldest Park, at least someone has likely been there before you.

Keewaydin 16

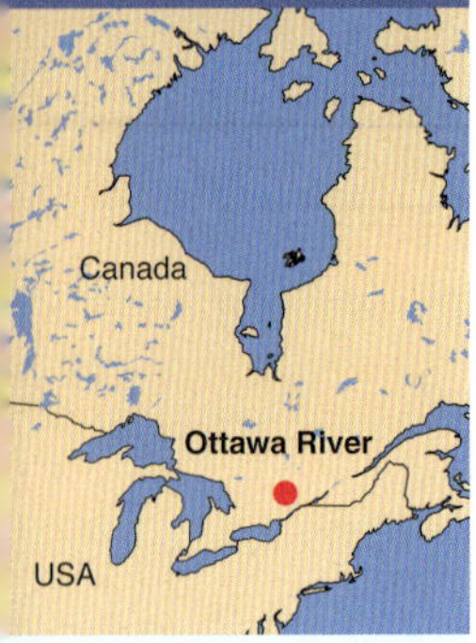


**Experience**
Intermediate – Expert

**Getting there**
Fly into Ottawa airport and hire a car

**In this location**
The Petawawa River and the Gatineau are nearby (by Canadian standards) and if you head over to Montreal you'll find the famous Lachine Rapids in the middle of the St Lawrence River

**On land**
The exciting city of Ottawa is just a few hours away, for a bit of urban action. Or the many outdoor outfitters in the area offer rafting, mountain biking and hiking options

# OTTAWA RIVER, CANADA

## Catching a ride on the freestyle bus!

It's no accident that the Ottawa has played host to the World Freestyle Championships and been the star destination in a plethora of glossy kayaking movies. Its variety of river features and differing water levels, and endless opportunities for play mean that the Ottawa is perfectly suited as a destination for kayakers looking for a relaxed, warm-weather trip with world-class whitewater. Whether you are an intermediate river runner, a big water hero or a top-level freestyle kayaker looking for the perfect waves to launch you into the air then the Ottawa has something sweet for you.

The river has a huge catchment area, which can mean some big variations in water levels. But high or low, the Ottawa delivers, as one feature starts to fade another comes into condition. The river is pool drop in nature, but the size and volume of the Ottawa can come as a shock to those not used to such big rivers, you could be forgiven for mistaking some of the large flat sections in between the awesome whitewater as lakes!

The action kicks off at the intimidating McCoy's Chute, home to Babyface, Corner Wave and the powerful hydraulic Horseshoe. Below here the river splits into two channels: the Main and the Middle. So named because the Main has the biggest flows and the Middle sits in the middle of all the islands in this section of river. The Main is all about BIG holes and huge, towering waves that build and crash with powerful force. The most famous of these is Bus Eater, a magnet for freestyling aerial specialists. So fast is the water that they use a makeshift waterski line to swing out into the current and hitch a ride on the bus-eating beast. Adrenaline surging, muscles taught, riding it feels like surfing an avalanche, but the skilled and the brave use the waves' size and dynamic nature to literally make their kayaks fly!

There's plenty more to keep you buzzing on your way down this river-running rollercoaster. Long rapid after long rapid will have you craning your neck at every horizon line. Lorne, Push Button, Butcher Knife, Lunch Stop Waves, Normans, Coliseum, Dog Leg and Blacks, they'll all have you hooting like a goon and heading up to run the whole thing again and again.

The Middle channel slices through a myriad of islands and has a more remote feel to it. Its character is different too with a more twisting, technical feel. Its rapids are pure quality though with highlights being Butterfly, Angel's Kiss, Garvin's Chute, Lower Garvin, Rollercoaster, Rock and Roll and the sweetly smooth, Black Velvet.

With it's variety of play spots and classic rapids you will never get bored of the Ottawa, it's a run that delivers, it's a pure fun, ultimate whitewater playground every time. Awesome!

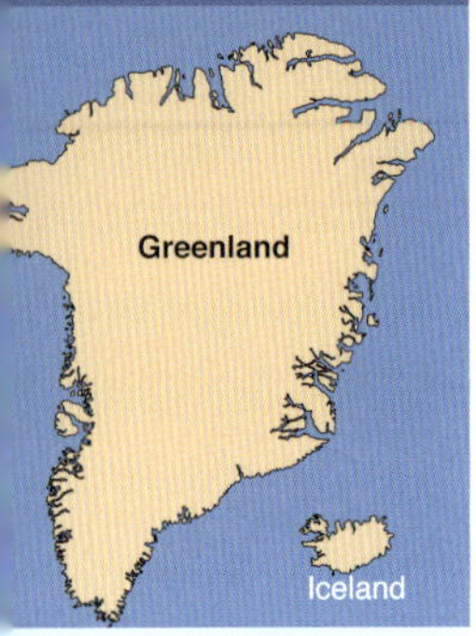


**Grade**
3-5

**Experience**
Expert

**Getting there**
Fly to one of Greenland's several international airports, then rent a 4X4 to drive as far as you can, hitch a lift on a fishing boat and then hike. Thorough pre-planning will be necessary to stand a chance of a successful kayaking mission in Greenland

**In this location**
There are many whitewater rivers to explore, you could go sea kayaking or you could visit or even participate in the Greenland national kayaking championships, an event that tests the skills of traditional Inuit sea kayakers

**On land**
Greenland is home to the world's largest National Park; go hiking or fishing, visit glaciers and ice floes or go dog sledding, there is plenty for the adventurous tourist to enjoy in Greenland

# INLAND RIVERS, GREENLAND

## Paddling off the map

There are many places on Earth that combine magnificent scenery and the raw power of nature but few do it on the scale of Greenland. The world's largest island boasts vast swathes of wilderness that present paddlers with exceptional freedom and testing challenges in equal measure. A population of just 57,000 inhabit an area of 840,000 square miles (2.17 million km$^2$), though more than three quarters of the country is covered by an ice cap more than 2 miles (3.2km) thick.

That's a lot of ice, and when it melts, there's a lot of water. No wonder that the unknown rivers of Greenland are the next big quest for whitewater explorers. Prehistoric granite bedrock combined with glacial meltwater produce big volume rivers with long slides, all hidden away in the Arctic wilderness.

Simply getting to the source of a river is an adventure in itself: a combination of hitching lifts on fishing boats and then hiking with all your equipment over the barren terrain is the only option to reach the source of many rivers. A British kayaking expedition in 2007 spent three days hiking into a river that didn't even have a name and the put-in was at the edge of the polar ice cap!

With so many incredible rivers in Greenland, it is hard to describe them all in detail, but there are, however, many similarities. The melting snow and glaciers feed huge amounts of very cold water into the rivers. The landscape is generally steep and the combination of the granite bedrock, steep relief and huge water volume creates formidable rapids, waterfalls and slides.

As if this wasn't enough to challenge those brave enough to attempt it, these rapids must all be negotiated with kayaks heavily laden with expedition supplies, food, shelter and emergency supplies. Due to the remote nature of whitewater kayaking, paddlers must rely on themselves and their buddies to be completely self-sufficient, help is often hundreds of miles away.

Whitewater expedition paddling in Greenland is no holiday; the lack of river descriptions, the lack of a transport network, the tundra environment and the sheer remoteness of everything rate Greenland as one of the toughest places on Earth to go whitewater kayaking.

**Experience**
Expert

**Getting there**
Most people fly into Narsarsuaq when travelling to Greenland, often via Reykjavik, Iceland. From there, hop on a flight to Kulusuk Island/Constable Point in East Greenland, where you can begin the boat logistics for the rest of your journey

**In this location**
Another popular area for sea kayaking is located slightly further north around Scoresby Sund, the largest fjord system in the world (for best access, it requires a boat shuttle)

**On land**
In the capital city of Nuuk, take time to visit the Greenland National Museum, as well as the wooden cathedral. If you can get to the Narsaq/Uunartoq region, sample its many hot springs and waterfalls (try the popular Nanortalik hiking route)

# SERMILIGAAQ-TASIILAQ FJORD, GREENLAND

## Fjords, glaciers and wilderness await in the Far North

If you want wildness with your wilderness, it doesn't get any more remote than sea kayaking in Greenland, the largest island in the world, which serves up pristine arctic fjords, glaciers and wildlife under polar skies as far north as you're likely to ever dip a paddle blade.

Also called Kalaallit Nunaat, Greenland offers countless options for sea kayakers pining for an arctic expedition. One of more popular is the Sermiligaaq-Tasiilaq fjord region in the country's eastern region, which is easier to access than the western coast due to flight connections through Iceland. While the eastern side still requires a fair amount of logistics, you're rewarded with one of the most unique paddling environments in the world.

Foremost, be prepared to paddle amongst ice. The area is rife with rock-pulverising glaciers that descend from the mountains to the sea, making boating among icebergs a daily occurrence. You'll get good at weaving in and around them, as well as scattered islands, as you progress deeper into each steep, rocky fjord. Camps might be hard to find (occasionally you might find yourself staying at an old Inuit encampment), but at 70 degrees latitude, there's plenty of daylight to keep paddling until you do.

On the wildlife front, expect to see everything from seals and whales (including narwhal, minke and fin) to arctic fox, musk ox and arctic hare. While the chance of seeing a polar bear is rare, they occur in the area also. The flora is equally unique, letting you camp among colorful arctic flowers, ground blueberries and mushrooms indigenous to the far north. Plan some time to also enjoy the region's hiking, which offers vast views of the surrounding fjordlands and peaks.

You'll have plenty of culture with your kayaking as well. More than half of Greenland's residents are Inuit, and you'll likely befriend residents of remote Inuit settlements as you go, most of whom will be as eager to learn about your ways as you are about theirs.

One trip frequented by outfitters heads out on a two-hour boat ride from Kulusuk Island to Tasiilaq, the administrative centre of Eastern Greenland. There, you can visit the local museum and overnight in a guest house before hiring a boat to drop you off in Sermiligaaq Fjord, part of the remote Tasiilaq fjord complex. Depending on your time and itinerary, from there you can paddle towards Ammassalik Fjord and the Knud Rasmussen Glacier. Longer trips can re-supply in such villages as Kummiut before meeting a pre-scheduled boat pick-up for the return ride to Kulusuk.

While weather conditions are relatively stable in summer, the area's ruggedness and isolation require being prepared for anything Mother Nature can muster. Wind can careen off the glaciers without notice, making crossings difficult. But as with glaciers, gales are all part of the package when it comes to paddling Greenland – and so is an experience you'll remember for a lifetime.

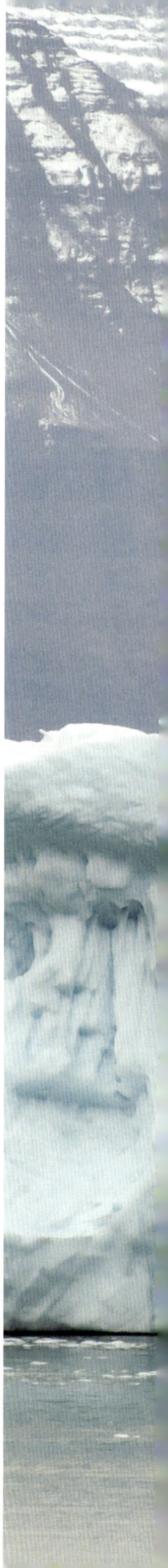

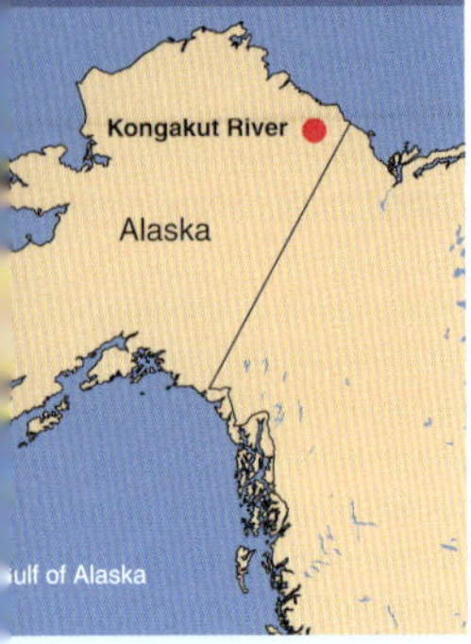


**Experience**
Intermediate – Expert

**Getting there**
Fly from Anchorage to Fairbanks and from there to Arctic Village, where you'll catch a bush flight to the headwaters

**In this location**
If you want more paddling in the Arctic, try the Class 2-3 Alatna River in Gates of the Arctic National Park, offering views of the Yosemite-like Arrigetch peaks towering over August tundra in full gold and red. Another great option: the Noatak, near the headwaters in Gates of the Arctic National Park to Kotzebue Sound

**On land**
Stay as long as you can to take advantage of the trip's great hikes, including a classic near the take-out that takes you up a long ridgeline where you can see the coastal plain

# KONGAKUT RIVER, ALASKA, USA

## The ultimate wildlife and wilderness experience

If you've ever wanted to canoe among caribou, head to the Kongakut River in the Brooks Range of Alaska, which offers the world's best opportunity to view the migration of thousands of caribou through the Arctic National Wildlife Refuge.

If your timing's right, you'll see animal representatives of the 13,000-strong porcupine caribou herd flow like the water in the river you're paddling, filing over hilltop after hilltop in one continual motion. Each year they migrate from wintering grounds in Canada's Yukon Territory to their calving grounds on Alaska's northern coastal plain. You'll likely be so breathtaken by one of nature's most incredible scenes that you'll forget, for a brief moment, the beauty of the rest of your surroundings: the 30,600-square-mile (80,000km$^2$) Arctic National Wildlife Refuge. It won't take you long to appreciate that as well.

Located in the heart of the refuge, the Kongakut is a multi-day canoeing and rafting classic, taking you 85 miles (137km) through some of the last unspoilt wilderness on earth. From headwaters to your take-out on the Beaufort Sea, you'll traverse the full range of arctic ecosystems, from the Romanoff Mountains to foothills, the coastal plain, coastal estuary and offshore barrier reefs of the Beaufort Sea. Known as the 'Serengeti of the north,' it also offers some of the best wildlife viewing on the planet. As well as caribou you'll likely see wolves, Dall sheep, grizzly bears, foxes and even musk ox and wolverine. The region is also rich with bird life, with more than 70 species summering in the Kongakut valley, from peregrine falcons and Lapland longspurs to Pacific, Arctic and red-throated loon. The region also harbours the highest concentration of nesting golden eagles in all of Alaska. And the safari doesn't end when you reach the Beaufort Sea and you dip your paddle in the Arctic Ocean on the far northern edge of North America. In the summer, when the ocean's icepack melts back from the shore, ringed seals as well as beluga bowhead whales often pass near the coast en route to their feeding grounds. You might also see prints from polar bears.

Of course, all this wilderness comes with a price, mainly in the form of time. If Alaska is hard to get to, you have to tack on three more flights from Anchorage, each one progressively 'bushier', just to get to the headwaters. Because of these flights, most private paddlers opt to do the trip in either inflatable canoes or kayaks for their packability and gear-hauling capability. Both options are fine for the waterway's Class 1-2 water, with an occasional Class 3.

To take best advantage of the region's 24 hours of daylight, high water and peak caribou viewing, the best time to run it is in June. Most parties take 10 to 12 days to travel the river's 85 miles (137km). Word of warning: be prepared for all types of weather – rain, snow, sun and wind – as well as mosquitoes, which are largely responsible for making the caribou migrate north to give birth.

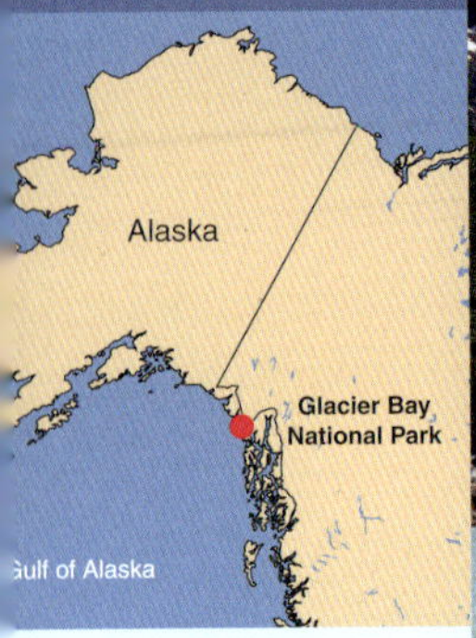


**Experience**
Intermediate – Expert

**Getting there**
There are only two ways to get to the Glacier Bay National Park gateway town of Gustavus: plane or boat. You can catch both out of Juneau

**In this location**
Just 15 miles (24km) away across Icy Strait lies Pt Adolphus on Chicagof Island, which is where to head if you want to paddle with whales. Sharing the waters with minkies and orcas, a pod of more than 25 humpbacks shows up each summer after wintering in Hawai'i

**On land**
If it's clear, take a charter flight tour to see the bay's glaciers and the nearby Juneau icefield. It's a land of extremes. In 1986, the Hubbard Glacier, just north of the bay, surged forward half a mile (0.8km) in two days, completely blocking off the entrance to Russell Fjord and trapping countless marine animals behind a wall of ice

# GLACIER BAY NATIONAL PARK, ALASKA, USA

## Paddling the land of ice

When the US bought Alaska from Russia in 1867 for $7.2 million, or roughly two cents an acre, the purchase included more than 30,000 square miles (78,000km$^2$) of glaciers – more than half of all the glaciers in the world – and resulted in 15 national parks totalling 85,000 square miles (220,000km$^2$). Combining two of these parks is Glacier Bay National Park – whose fjords and 16 tidewater glaciers were declared a national monument in 1925 and a World Heritage site in 1992.

A scant 250 years ago, the entire bay was blocked off by a massive 5,000-foot-thick (1524m) wall of ice. When Captain George Vancouver sailed by in 1794, the bay's main glacier was just six miles (9.7km) past the entrance to the bay. When John Muir came back 85 year later, it had retreated 48 miles (77km) up the bay. Now, nearly 140 years after Muir arrived, it's retreated more than 65 miles (105km), exposing a glacier and mountain-lined fjord where you can dip your paddle blade for days.

Lying just 60 miles (97km) north-west of Alaska's capital of Juneau, the region offers 16 tidewater

glaciers to explore – including such classics as Riggs, McBride and Muir. You can camp right near their faces, chipping off thousands-of-years-old glacier ice from icebergs for your post-paddle cocktails, while listening to their incessant rumblings around the campfire.

The park has two main arms for exploring, all filled with such Alaskan wildlife as whales, porpoise, seals, bears and eagles. On a clear day, as you slalom through icebergs en route to taking in the next commanding wall of ice, it's hard not to crane your neck skyward. The bay's glaciers are surrounded by the tallest coastal mountains in the world, including 15,300-foot (4,663m) Mt Fairweather. You'll also see Nunatak, a long rocky green pyramid that Muir saw sticking out of a sea of ice that's now surrounded by water.

While you can start paddling from Bartlett Cove just outside the town of Gustavus, it'll take you a couple of days to get up to the ice. Many paddlers opt to catch a ride further up the fjord on the daily tour boat (camper orientation meeting and backcountry registration form required beforehand), and then get picked up again at a certain time and place for the shuttle bus back to Gustavus.

If you have to wait for your pick-up, bring a copy of Muir's *Travels to Alaska*, where you can read about the first time he visited the bay: 'At length the clouds lifted and beneath their gray fringes I saw the berg-filled expanse of the bay, and the feel of the mountains that stand about it, and the imposing fronts of five huge glaciers. This was my first view of Glacier Bay, a solitude of ice and snow and newborn rocks, dim, dreary and mysterious.'

**Grade**
3-4

**Experience**
Expert

**Getting there**
Fly to Anchorage and then either hop on a bush flight or drive north to Talkeetna (about a four-hour drive). From there you need to hire a bush plane to fly your party and gear to the put-in

**In this location**
Spend time to paddle other classics in the region, including the Lion's Head run of the Matanuska, the Nenana near Denali National Park, and Sixmile Creek an hour out of Anchorage

**On land**
You're close to Denali, so hire a bush plane from Talkeetna Air Taxi to fly you over the Alaskan Range and 9,400-square-mile (24,300km$^2$) Denali National Park, with a snow landing on the Kahiltna Glacier

# TALKEETNA RIVER, ALASKA, USA

## The best multi-day whitewater in the state

Billed as the best all-around whitewater river in Alaska, the Talkeetna River, located in the shadow of 20,320-foot (6193m) Denali / Mount McKinley, serves up whitewater and wilderness in heaping big Alaskan portions.

The four- to five-day, 60-mile (97km) trip through the Talkeetna Mountains requires a bush flight from the remote town of Talkeetna, known as the 'Gateway to Denali', but you're rewarded for the extra logistical hassles with one of the finest wilderness whitewater trips in the hemisphere.

While kayakers often put in on Murder Lake to float Class 2, bear-filled Prairie Creek seven miles (11km) to the confluence with the Talkeetna, rafters most often fly another 22 miles (35km) upstream to a gravel bar three miles (5km) below Yellowjacket Creek. Wherever you start, as soon as the plane leaves from its final lap shuttling your group and gear and you're left alone on the river's cobblestone banks in the middle of nowhere, the reality of your insignificance sets in. Surrounding you are the rolling, forested hills of the Talkeetnas, and behind them the mighty and towering Alaskan Range, with nary a road for more than 70 miles (113km) in all directions. The solitude, wilderness and wildlife are striking.

For rafters putting in on the upper Talkeetna, the first day or two will consist of fast-moving, Class 1-2,

shallow and braided water, where you can watch the scenery pass by as if on a giant escalator through the wilderness. You'll likely see bear, moose and caribou on the banks between patches of willow, cottonwood and spruce, and warblers and eagles floating on thermals high above. After a day or two you'll come to Prairie Creek, best avoided from mid-July to mid-August when salmon spawn, drawing in bears. You'll see salmon carcasses lining the creek bottom and shore, while those still spawning fight their way upstream.

Seven miles (11km) downstream is the crown jewel, where the wilderness gives way to whitewater. Rounding a bend, you'll see the canyon narrow as its granite walls are squeezed between two riverside cliffs. Get your game face on as this marks the beginning of nearly 15 miles (24km) of non-stop Class 3-4 wilderness rapids. The stretch leads off with a bang. Just below the first horizon line is a rapid called Entrance Exam, a large hole followed by a right-hand turn into a boulder-filled stretch punctuated by Toilet Bowl and Sluice Box (scout the entire rapid on the right by climbing to an overlook on the cliff). One glance down is all it takes to discover that Class 4 in the wilderness takes on a whole new meaning.

The rapids continue non-stop afterward for one of the best whitewater days you'll experience anywhere. After being spat out of the 15-mile-long (24km) canyon, you'll finally get to relax with a 33-mile (53km) float below Iron Creek to your take-out back in Talkeetna, where the river joins forces with the even larger Susitna, which hides notorious Devil's Canyon upstream.

From there, it's off to a beer and burger at either the Talkeetna Roadhouse or Denali Brewing Company to share your tales.

**Grade**
3-4

**Experience**
Intermediate

**Getting there**
International flights come into Las Vegas. From there you'll transfer to Flagstaff and then drive out to Lee's Ferry. Full descents of the Canyon begin at Lee's Ferry, although it is possible to start lower down at the Phantom Ranch for a shorter trip

**In this location**
If you're still keen to paddle after your time on the Grand then Arizona has a lot of different whitewater rivers. The Little Colorado, Black River, Verde River and Salt River all have sections of quality whitewater

**On land**
Cycling, walking and mule trips along the rim of the Canyon are common, or you can even take a helicopter flight over the Grand

# GRAND CANYON, ARIZONA, USA

## The most famous river trip in the world!

The Grand Canyon was first explored by boat by John Wesley Powell in 1869. On that historic trip Powell travelled with nine men and four wooden dory boats and took ten months to complete his journey. These days it takes about 12 days to paddle the 277 miles (446km) to the finish, dropping 1,079 feet (329m) along the way.

Because of the time it takes the best way to run the Canyon in a kayak or canoe is to have an accompanying oar raft to carry all the kit, food and beer that you'll need. A permit is needed to run a private trip on the Grand. The other option is to pay to go on a commercial trip with a licensed operator.

The journey begins at Lee's Ferry, and the history of the place literally hangs in the air. The anticipation, excitement and fear of 200 years' worth of adventures buzz around the rocks. Hopes and dreams drift down with the current. Many who have departed from that spot were never to make it to Lake Mead, at the foot of the river, and many arrive there changed forever by the experience.

The named rapids are too numerous to list here, over 150, but just hearing names such as Granite, Hermit, Crystal and Lava Falls will get the blood pumping. Since the Glen Canyon Dam was built the river runs emerald green at the start but, as the water level rises and its tributaries feed in, it becomes a thick, muddy maelstrom. The feeling as you thunder down a steep green tongue at a rapid like Crystal or Lava, towards one of the biggest holes that you've ever seen is indescribable. Your boat bucks underneath you as it rides the huge humps of whitewater, like riding rodeo on the back of a giant, crazy, mud-coloured, watery stallion. The feeling of jubilation at making it through such a monster in one piece is overwhelming. Many commercial groups hold ABL (Alive Below Lava) parties at a certain campsite to celebrate.

A trip down the Grand isn't just about the river though. You are travelling though a place of staggering natural beauty. Leave the river behind and take the time to hike up and explore some of its side canyons. You won't be disappointed as you marvel at its geological grandeur, but remember to watch out for canyon rattlers as you climb!

Whether on a private or a commercial trip, a journey down the Grand is a shared experience too, as you and your fellow river runners work as a team to get everyone safely to the bottom, enjoying every precious second of the journey through one of the most amazing places on earth.

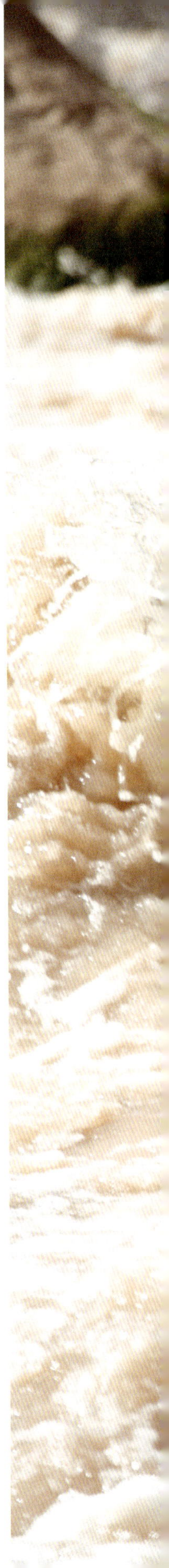

**Grade**
1-3

**Experience**
Novice

**Getting there**
From Little Rock, get to Harrison as a starting point. To reach the Upper District, head south on Highway 7, or Highway 43. To reach the Middle District, travel 31 miles (50km) south on Highway 65. To reach the Lower District take Highway 65 south from Harrison for 5 miles (8km), then Highway 62/412 east to Yellville, and Highway 14 south

**In this location**
Bring your fishing rod and head to the nearby Little Red River. For whitewater, hit the wild & scenic Mulberry, offering 50 miles (80km) of Class 2-3 from its home in the Ozarks to its confluence with the Arkansas

**On land**
Visit Blanchard Springs Cavern for a cave fix

# BUFFALO RIVER, ARKANSAS, USA

## A haven for canoeists of all abilities

Of Arkansas's more than 90,000 miles (144,840km) of rivers, streams and bayous, the Buffalo National River represents its heart and soul. Becoming America's first national river in 1972, the 135-mile (217km) long, free-flowing waterway offers both swift-running and placid stretches, whose beaches, gravel bars, bluffs, woodlands and 148 square miles (383km$^2$) of protected wilderness make it one of the best canoeing runs in the country.

One of the few remaining rivers in the lower 48 states without dams, the Buffalo cuts its way through massive limestone bluffs as it flows eastward through the Arkansas Ozarks and into the White River. But perhaps its best attribute is its suitability for paddlers of all levels and ease of access. The upper stretches harbour just enough mild whitewater at normal flows to keep you on your toes, while the middle and lower reaches offer mellower sections for the whole family. You can bring your own canoe or rent one from a variety of local outfitters and liveries.

The river in the long, narrow park is crossed by three highways, but its length ensures plenty of solitude. You can camp at one of the park's 13 designated campgrounds spaced all along the length

of the river (make reservations at www.recreation.gov), which range from primitive to those with full hook-ups, and venture out on day trips, or pack your gear with you and spend the night on a gravel bar, a favourite local pastime. Those looking to sleep off the ground can also stay in cabins constructed by the Civilian Conservation Corps.

Typically, the float season begins in the spring, whose higher water levels attract canoeists looking to hone skills on moderate whitewater. Flows subside throughout the summer, making it suitable to paddlers of all levels.

Still, rainfall can change levels overnight, so pay attention to forecasts, camp above the high water mark and pull your boats up at night. More than one party has come home with tales of being stranded by rising water.

You can also use the waterway to hone your native heritage skills. Native Americans lived within the Buffalo valley on terraces and under the massive bluffs lining the waterway. You can even take time from your trip to hike to the bluff shelter known as Indian Rockhouse, as well as Hemmed-In-Hollow Falls, at 204 feet (62m) the tallest wet-weather waterfall in the Midwest.

Side trips aside, the real reason to run the river is its reputation as one of the best canoeing runs in the country and the cornerstone of the new Arkansas Water Trails programme, which links urban and rural paddling routes throughout the state. And it earns all of these accolades in a state whose paddling options are outnumbered only by its crayfish.

**Experience**
Novice

**Getting there**
Fly into Tampa and take Highway 19 north to the town of Fanning Springs. Base out of there or the town of Suwannee, which marks the trail's end

**In this location**
To paddle with manatees head to the Homosassa and Crystal rivers near Homosassa, (launch at Homosassa River Resort marina). The best viewing months are December and January when they feed on aquatic plants in shallow, spring-fed rivers

**On land**
The confluence of the Suwannee River estuary and Gulf of Mexico creates a rich wildlife environment with more than 250 bird species, all protected by the Lower Suwannee Wildlife Refuge. You can also hike or bike the Dixie Mainline Trail, which heads north from Suwannee paralleling the coastline

# BIG BEND PADDLING TRAIL, FLORIDA, USA

## Sea kayaking the Big Bend

Want to paddle an easy-to-follow, warm-water and -weather water trail? Head to Florida, a state that pioneered the United States' water trail concept featuring a linked set of campsites and mapped routes for paddling trips of all lengths.

It's easy to see why the state has such a legacy. The Sunshine State's wealth of tranquil, protected waters combined with swamps, saltwater keys, barrier islands and gin-clear freshwater springs make it unparallelled for paddling opportunities, ranging from canoe trails in the interior to sea kayaking routes along the Gulf's inside passage.

Perhaps the crown jewel of all of these is the Big Bend Saltwater Paddling Trail along the section of Gulf Coast shoreline curving from the panhandle to the peninsula's northern reaches. The 105-mile (169km) trail, which parallels one of the longest and wildest publicly owned coastal wetlands in the United States, offers bays and barrier islands to explore, as well as side-trips to freshwater springs and hiking trails to stretch your legs after the day's paddle.

As well as your conventional boating and camping gear, make sure to bring your binoculars. The section is known for its rich variety of bird life. On a typical outing you can expect to see everything from eagles and egrets to pelicans and osprey.

Wildlife diversity is equally world class in the water, just on a slightly larger scale. Kayakers can expect to see sea turtles and rays gliding beneath their hulls, as well as massive manatees, which also call the area home.

Most trips head north to south from the Aucilla River to the trail's end at Salt Creek Landing in the town of Suwannee. To escape the heat and the bugs, the best time to paddle the trail is from early December through March, though it's open from September through June. It's also best to tackle it in sea kayaks; afternoon winds can create white caps and rough water, which can wash over the gunwales of canoes.

Plan to spend at least a week to paddle its full length. You'll also need a permit, and don't expect to search out campsites on your own. Regulations require you to stay at one of seven designated campsites en route, each one spaced 10 to 14 miles (16 to 23km) apart, with one or two nights at private sites. You can also do shorter excursions, including day trips or one of three different three-day-long permitted trips. For additional information, get a $19.75 copy of the 40-page, water-resistant *Big Bend Saltwater Paddling Trail Guide*, which contains natural and cultural information as well as compass bearings, and maps with GPS points and mileage markers for locating campsites as well as side-trips, trails, historical sites and other points of interest.

**Grade**
5

**Experience**
Expert

**Getting there**
Get to Boise however you can. From there head up Highway 55 toward Banks and Cascade. The Lower Five will be on your left and the middle and upper sections will be on your right

**In this location**
If you're in the area, you might as well notch a few other Idaho classics. Right next door is the South Fork Payette and a short drive takes you to such Idaho mainstays as the Secesh/South Fork of the Salmon, Middle Fork, Selway and more

**On land**
Kill time in the city by hiking or biking Boise's 25-mile-long (40km) Green Belt trail or visiting The Peregrine Fund's World Center for Birds of Prey on 0.6 square miles ($1.6km^2$) south of town on Cole Road. If you're a sports buff and you're boating in the autumn, try to take in a Boise State football game at Bronco Stadium

# PAYETTE RIVER, IDAHO, USA

## Test your mettle on the North Fork

Cascading through a maze of road construction and railroad debris, Idaho's North Fork of the Payette runs 15 miles (24km) from Smith's Ferry to the town of Banks. This constant Class 5 whitewater has tested the mettle – and launched the careers – of some of the sport's best.

Generations of boaters have used the North Fork as a testing ground, including such pioneers and paddling legends as Walt Blackadar, Doug Ammons, Jon Wasson, Rob Lesser, Grant Amaral, Scott Lindgren, Charlie Munsey and Gerry Moffatt. Many of these kayakers earned their stripes here before going on to make big names for themselves in the world of whitewater.

Not that you don't make your name simply by paddling – and surviving – the North Fork. Careening alongside the highway – where you can get out to scout nearly every drop, incurring butterflies in the process – the 15-mile (24km) stretch features three sections of varying Class 5 difficulty. While releases from a dam upstream keep traditional summer flows hovering around 2,000 cubic feet ($56m^3$), it's known to rise with run-off, increasing both its power and difficulty, peaking around 10,000 cubic feet ($280m^3$), keeping all but the bravest boaters at bay. For good reason. Even at milder flows the stretch has killed some of the sport's best, including the likes of Lucas Turner, Richard Carson, Conrad Fourney and Boyce Greer.

Most paddlers opt to test the relatively tamer waters of the Lower Five first; while still Class 5, the rapids – including such classic big-water wave trains as Hounds Tooth, Otters Slide, Juicer and Crunch – are a bit more straightforward than their Class 5 cousins upstream.

Once boaters are comfortable with the river's power in this section, they head up river. Next on the pecking order is the Upper Five, with such rapids as Steepness, Nutcracker (the section's premier drop), Disneyland and S-Turn. Big Eddy, the North Fork's only real flatwater, separates the Upper from the Middle. It's the middle section that truly puts the North Fork on the map with the most powerful, continuous whitewater. Here, such rapids as Jacob's Ladder – the last rapid run during the upper section's first descent in 1977 – lead straight into a half-mile (0.8km) stretch of chaos known as the Golf Course (named for all its holes) and Jaws.

As well as its continuous whitewater, which plunges 1,700 vertical feet (518m) in just 15 miles (24km), the stretch boasts warm water that comes off the top of the dam, has flows that extend well into the autumn, and offers roadside scouting and 'safety' the entire way. Get good enough on it and you can try to run a vertical mile of whitewater by making three top-to-bottom runs in a day. Ammons once even did five top-to-bottoms for 8,500 vertical feet (2,590m) of Class 5 in a day. Do so and you'll likely fall asleep at one of several roadside camping areas along Highway 55 before your helmeted head even hits your pillow.

Kokatat
Kokatat
Dagger

**Experience**
Novice

**Getting there**
Your best bet for either trip is to fly into either Bangor International or Hancock County-Bar Harbor airports and plot your driving route from there. Access the St John put-in by driving to Millinocket, then 100 miles (161km) on the Golden Road to Baker Lake (you can also floatplane in from Ambadjejus Lake). For the St Croix, you need to drive north to Vanceboro

**In this location**
Try an 85-mile (137km) canoe trip down the Machias river (Native American for bad run of water), a free-flowing river running through one of the largest tracts of woodlands in the eastern United States

**On land**
Since you're in the area, hit a portion of the fabled Appalachian Trail, 281 miles (452km) of which are in Maine with its terminus at Mt Katahdin, the highest point in the state, in Baxter State Park

# ST CROIX & ST JOHN RIVERS, MAINE, USA

## Paddling the pine-tree state

Maine is canoe country, and if you're not convinced, head to the St Croix and St John rivers, where you'll quickly become a convert. Designated as a Canadian Heritage River, meaning no further development will take place on either shore, the St Croix forms the boundary between Maine and New Brunswick, Canada, draining 1,500 square miles (3,900km$^2$) before ending in the Bay of Fundy. Canoeists wishing to tackle just the river portion launch in Vanceboro and take three to four days to paddle down to Kellyland. It is as quintessential a canoeing trip as you'll find anywhere.

And don't worry about finding a great place to camp. Strategically located campsites are placed just where you need them, complete with such amenities as toilets and picnic tables. The river's difficulty progression is just as well coordinated. It lets you get your feet wet, so to speak, with a long flatwater section, before the gradient and current picks up into a slightly harder quick-water section. Master this and it's on to easy, pool-drop Class 2 rapids – just difficult enough to force you and your partner to

coordinate efforts.

The climax is Little Falls, which is easily scouted. If you think your skills are up to it, you can run your boat loaded. If not, you can portage your gear and run your boat empty – that way the only consequence of swamping or flipping is you going in the drink. And if you don't want anything to do with it, you can always portage.

You can take out at Loon Bay if you want to shorten the trip by a day, but you still have to face Canoose Ledges, which is easy to scout and portage on the left bank. Continue on and the gradient eases into a final stretch of flatwater that carries you to the dam at your take-out at Kellyland.

The St John offers a similar Maine canoeing experience. The longest free-flowing river east of the Mississippi, the St John meanders through several headwater lakes and then on for more than another 100 miles (161km) through forests, rolling hills and open valleys.

The best and most popular stretch is a 100-mile (161km), six- to seven-day trip from Baker Lake to Allagash Village, where large portions of the shore are owned by The Nature Conservancy. From Baker Lake you'll start your trip by following the river as it winds through dense forests of spruce and fir, dodging occasional rocks and negotiating slow but steady ripples. The two main rapids of note are Big Black and Big Rapids, both of which should be scouted. As with the St Croix, the stretch's campsites are well spaced and maintained, and the perfect place to blow steam off your coffee and settle into a stack of Maine blueberry pancakes with Maine maple syrup.

**Experience**
Novice

**Getting there**
From Boston take I-95 north to Augusta, Maine, then Route 3 east to Ellsworth and on to Mount Desert Island. You can also fly into the Hancock County Airport, located 10 miles (16km) from the park, or Bangor, located just an hour away

**In this location**
Maine also has a wealth of rivers, both whitewater and tranquil. For a rapids fix, head to the nearby Penobscot or Kennebec

**On land**
Road trip. Drive the 20-mile (32km) Park Loop Road and 3.5-mile (5.6km) road up Cadillac Mountain; there's also a short hiking loop atop the mountain where you can stretch your sea kayak-atrophied legs

# ACADIA NATIONAL PARK, MAINE, USA

## The gem of the Maine Island Trail

Following 325 miles (523km) of pristine Maine coast, the Maine Island Trail, created in 1993 and passing directly through Acadia National Park near Penobscot, was the first water trail created in the USA. It has become popular for good reason. It offers paddlers a chance to explore portions of the state's 3,478 miles (5,597km) of coastline and islands, with pre-established launch points and campsites in protected bays. And the crowning feature of the trail is Acadia, near the sea kayak Mecca of Bar Harbor.

Established in 1916 as the first National Park east of the Mississippi, the park is located along the coast of 'Downeast' Maine and consists of 64 square miles (166km$^2$) of rock-bound shoreline on Mount Desert Island, a portion of the Schoodic Peninsula and numerous offshore islands.

All this makes it a sea kayaker's dream. While many come to hike the park's granite mountains and pristine lakes, a paddling trip is even better, providing a unique view of all things Maine, from marine life to the island's rocky western coast and Cadillac Mountain, the highest point on the East Coast. You'll also see where glaciers have carved through an east-west ridge of granite, leaving mountains and valleys much like the wake of your kayak. And if you hanker after more recent history, it offers that too,

letting you tour such historic sites as the Bass Harbor Head Lighthouse.

While guide services offer paddling tours in the park, if you're experienced you can tackle it relatively easily on your own. Public boat ramps are available in Bar Harbor, Northeast Harbor and Southwest Harbor, with additional access sites at Seal Cove, Bass Harbor, Seal Harbor Beach and Hadley Point. Many head straight to Frenchman Bay and Blue Hill bays for their commanding views of the coast.

You can also base your paddling trip out of the quaint town of Bar Harbor, taking day trips and then returning to town for cosy, Maine charm. Nestled on the eastern shore of Mount Desert Island and flanked by granite cliffs and forested islands, the town offers a wealth of paddling options, from shoreline 'gunkholing' to open crossings.

Options include heading out from town at the low tide sandbar, touring Cranberry Isles at the mouth of Somes Sound (park at the public beach in Seal Harbor), and paddling the northern reaches of Frenchman Bay at Hadley Point. For an overnighter, park at Seal Cove and paddle north-west toward Long Island where the park protects the island from development.

Wherever you go, expect wildlife ... and weather. While you're likely to see everything from harbour porpoises and seals to bald eagles, osprey and seabirds, you'll also encounter varying conditions. Trouble comes easily in Maine's waters, where tides, rough seas, fog and cold water can test the mettle of even the most seasoned paddlers (especially watch the weather in Frenchman Bay). Know how to self-rescue and dress appropriately.

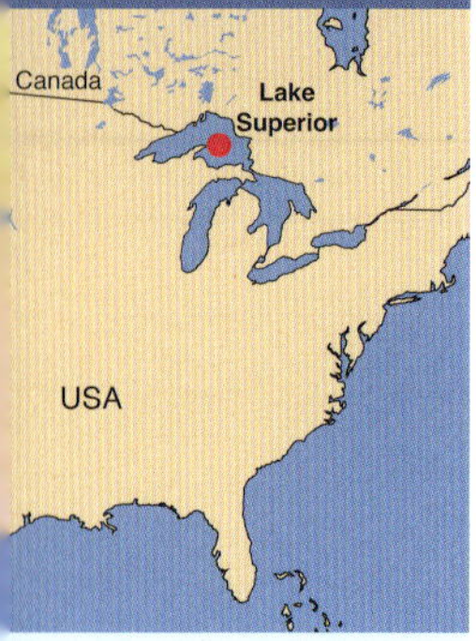


**Experience**
Intermediate – Expert

**Getting there**
Head for Munising, Michigan which is reachable by car, plane or boat. Paddle from there, or drive Highway 58 north-east to Sand Point towards Grand Marais

**In this location**
Lake Superior offers countless other paddling opportunities, including Isle Royale and the 45-mile (72km) Keweenaw Water Trail. But head to the Apostle Islands National Lakeshore near Bayfield, an archipelago of 21 islands and 12 miles (19km) of lakeshore known for its pristine shoreline and wilderness camping in old-growth forest

**On land**
Plan an extra day or two to stretch your legs along the Lakeshore Hiking Trail, which parallels your kayak route along the shore

# LAKE SUPERIOR, MICHIGAN, USA

## Sea kayak the multi-coloured marvel

While non-profits and government agencies have worked hard to create a 3,000-mile (4,828km) long water trail completely circling Lake Superior, the world's largest freshwater lake carved by glaciers from some of the oldest rock formations on earth, it's a short, 42-mile (68km) stretch on its southern reaches that often creates the most fanfare for paddlers. Lying along Lake Superior's southern edge, Pictured Rocks National Lakeshore offers some of North America's most picturesque paddling.

While the area offers 42 miles (68km) of shoreline, which includes the 300-feet (91m) high Grand Sable Dunes, it's a 15-mile (24km) stretch of coastline that makes you want to fish out your watercolour set. It's here that 500-million-year-old Cambrian sandstone cliffs rise anywhere from 50 to 200 feet (15 to 61m) straight up out of the water in a spectacular palette of colours pouring down the rock faces like paint.

The streaks of white, blue, orange, red and black come from the rock's manganese, iron, copper and limonite, minerals that will make you want to extend your stay for as long as possible. At sunset, the colours take on an even more vibrant hue as they mix with the green of the surrounding forest and blue of the lake.

To paddle the shoreline, it's best to start from Sand Point, the lakeshore's southernmost access point, and paddle to the northern harbour at Grand Marais. Most paddlers take up to four days to paddle the entire stretch.

While you'll be competing for campsites with hikers (there are 13 hike-in campsites and seven group sites along the Lakeshore Hiking Trail) paddlers can reserve them ahead of time, ensuring a place to pitch your tent after watching the colours at sunset. Permits are required and book up early, so it's advised to secure reservations beforehand.

As well as paddling the entire lakeshore, you can also take shorter routes and even head out for day-paddles that still take you to some of the most scenic destinations. One favourite is the 15-mile (24km) paddle from Miner's Castle to aptly named, 100-foot (30m) Spray Falls, which cascades into the lake in a huge bridal veil of water. You'll also want to take photos of Miner's Castle, a large sandstone formation looming over the water, and explore the many sea caves at its base. You can also paddle through a giant rock arch named Lover's Leap and stretch your legs on the fine sands of Mosquito Beach.

In short, the lakeshore offers everything you could want in a paddling trip, all condensed down into a 42-mile (68km) package containing everything from beaches and waterfalls to sea caves, dunes, arches and more.

# BOUNDARY WATERS, MINNESOTA, USA

## Wilderness the way it's supposed to be

**Experience**
Novice

**Getting there**
The nearest airport is in Duluth, which offers direct flights to most major cities in the US. From there, you can either rent a car or hire a shuttle for the three-hour, 140-mile (225km) drive along Lake Superior on MN Hwy 61 N to the Gunflint Trail entry point

**In this location**
Swap your canoe for a sea kayak and head out on the 150-mile (241km) Minnesota segment of the 3,000-mile (4,828km) long Lake Superior Water Trail, spanning the state's Lake Superior shoreline, from Duluth's St Louis Bay to the Pigeon River on the Canadian border

**On land**
Take the North Shore Scenic Drive along Lake Superior, and visit Viking-named Leif Erickson Park and the Lake Superior Maritime Museum

Rarely will you find a more pristine setting to dip a canoe blade than in the Boundary Waters, a 3,125-square-mile (8,090km$^2$) region of wilderness straddling the US / Canada border between Minnesota and Ontario just west of Lake Superior. From the echoing call of loons to dipping your cup over your gunwales to drink straight from the lake, the region offers everything you'd want in a multi-day canoe trip, and more.

Including part of Superior National Forest and Voyageurs National Park in north-eastern Minnesota, as well as La Verendrye and Quetico Provincial Parks in Ontario, the canoeing hotbed offers more solitude per stroke than you'll find anywhere else in the Lower 48. Much of that is due to its wilderness designation. The Boundary Waters Canoe Area Wilderness (BWCAW) was established in 1978, restricting logging, mining and most motorised access to more than 1,500 square miles (3,900km$^2$) in northern Minnesota.

And that's exactly what makes it so special. Visited by more than 150,000 visitors annually, the region offers more than 1,500 miles (2,114km) of canoe routes and more than 2,000 campsites – plenty of room to stretch your legs (and arms, after the day's paddle). Most of the paddling routes can be accessed via one of 60 official entry sites, most located near the towns of Ely and Grand Marais.

A typical day takes you through a glacially carved landscape, including lakes cut from Precambrian granite and surrounded by old-growth pine forests. When you come to a lake's end, you transfer onto a well-marked portage trail that leads you to the next lake on your route.

But don't plan to just show up and go – especially if you're planning an overnight outing. Because it's a wilderness area, you need a permit for your launch date and entry point (available at www.recreation.gov). To lower the impact of large groups, group sizes are limited to nine people and four watercraft. And plan ahead; some of the most popular entry points fill up months in advance.

Plan your route wisely also; don't plan a 25-mile-a-day (40km) itinerary if you're taking your grandmother and kids. And bear in mind the portages. Since the region is essentially a linked-together series of lakes, carrying your gear – and canoes – between waterways is part of the Boundary Waters package and cuts into time you'll make on the water.

If you're unfamiliar with multi-day canoe camping, choose from a variety of outfitters who will do everything for you. You can also rent your gear from one – including everything from canoes and paddles to camp chairs and stoves – and get advice on campsites and routes before striking out on your own.

**Grade**
5

**Experience**
Expert

**Getting there**
The upper Raven Fork is in the Great Smokey Mountains National Park, North Carolina, USA. The take-out for the run is in the Cherokee Reservation and you should ask permission from the local people to park and to paddle the river

**In this location**
The section of the Raven Fork that flows through the Reservation land is closed for paddlers. The south-east USA is jam packed with awesome canoeing for all levels, there is even an Olympic Canoe Slalom course on the Ocoee River from the 1996 Atlanta Games

**On land**
The Great Smokey Mountains National Park is an ideal place for all outdoor adventurers, from short walks to hiking tours lasting several days, fishing and even bear spotting, the Great Smokey Mountains offer it all

# RAVEN FORK RIVER, NORTH CAROLINA, USA

## No room for mistakes

The Raven Fork River is one of the most demanding whitewater canoeing adventures in one of the most remote and untouched valleys in south-east USA. It is a solid test for even the most accomplished whitewater warriors.

The first complete descent of the upper Raven Fork section was in March 1999. The upper Raven Fork flows into Cherokee Indian land and it is imperative to politely ask their permission before parking your vehicle at the take-out which is on the reservation at the home of Emmanuel. You will need a good pair of shoes and strong will as the adventure begins with a tough hike up one of the two routes to the put-in. The hike is a test of fitness and strength, even before you reach the water. The anticipation and the excitement start to build as you shoulder your canoe, leaving your truck behind and starting the long hike up towards the put-in. Heading downstream, you must take the time in the first mile and a half (2.4km) to soak up the scenery: the stream has a beautiful canopy of trees with limbs that snake all the way across the river. There are another few hundred yards before the action truly begins. Lightning quick reactions, brave decisions and strong arms are needed to blast over the bubbling whitewater, manoeuvre through the boulder-choked rapids and jump down the slides and drops that constantly challenge the brave riders. Lining up and dropping into the first rapid causes a mixture of feelings: 'Wow! I want more' combined with 'Oh my God this is insane.'

The Raven Fork is a steep Alpine-style river with numerous tricky rapids, slides and drops to test all aspects of the riders' skills: Lord of the Rings, Anaconda, Mortal Kombat and Mike Tyson's. Even the best will choose to carry around one or two of the hardest rapids on the river, the risk of making a mistake is just too great.

The Raven Fork is one of those special rivers that you can look down – it is that steep. The steepest mile starting at the aptly named Jedi Training which drops 764 feet (223m). The upper section of the Raven Fork is about 2.5 miles (4km) with pool drop style whitewater, a steep section of rapids followed by a flat pool before the next section of rapids.

Of course no trip to the Raven Fork would be complete without sharing a cold beer with Emmanuel at the take-out.

*Without Emmanuel's support there would be no access to the Raven Fork, thanks.*

**Experience**
Novice

**Getting there**
Get to Moab by bus, train or air (nearest airports are Canyonlands Field, Grand Junction & Salt Lake City). Heading north out of Moab will get you to various put-ins along the Colorado and Green Rivers. You can hire a shuttle to take you back the way you came

**In this location**
Try hiking or driving to take in the Islands in the Sky, The Maze and The Needles

**On land**
Spend some time to visit some of the other national parks in the area, including Arches and Capitol Reef, and, if time allows, Bryce and Zion a bit further away. In Arches, take the family-friendly hike to Delicate Arch, complete with a natural ramp traverse in the sandstone

# LABYRINTH & STILLWATER CANYONS, UTAH, USA

## Canoeing in the Canyonlands

You won't find a better place to get in touch with your inner Edward Abbey, author of such books as *Desert Solitaire* and *The Monkey Wrench Gang*, than a multi-day canoe trip through the heart of Canyonlands National Park on the Green River's Labyrinth and Stillwater canyons. You'll probably need a permit for boating and / or driving in the Park, so book before you go. This section of the Green offers 120 miles (193km) of rock-strewn splendour in which to immerse your soul in desert wilderness. Though it's as flat as the mesas atop the canyon cliffs, averaging a gradient of only 1.5 feet (0.5m) per mile, the run is popular among canoeists, sea kayakers and rafters looking to lose themselves in canyon country.

En route you'll find massive sandstone cliffs towering overhead, side canyons with superb hiking, and campsites littered with broad, sand beaches. It is essential to bring your own water, with experts recommending a gallon per person per day.

The canyons were named by John Wesley Powell during his journey in 1869, and the reason behind their monikers still holds true today. A maze of side canyons, grottos and arroyos appear after each new bend, the highlight of which is the aptly named Maze and Doll House on river right, best accessed from the Spanish Bottom campsite just below the river's confluence with the Colorado. Allow for an extra layover day to explore its winding passages.

There is, however, one important logistical matter to consider. Just below the confluence lies the torrent of Cataract Canyon, a Class 3-4 freight train of big water rapids that's no place for inexperienced paddlers (but is a great rafting run for those with the proper skills) that eventually dumps into Lake Powell. So when you reach the confluence of the Colorado, your only option is to meet a pre-arranged pick-up with a jet boat to motor you back up the Colorado – a journey worth the trip in itself as it whisks you up the other primary artery forming Canyonlands National Park. The other alternative is to just run Labyrinth Canyon and take out well upstream at Mineral Bottom, which is reachable by car. No matter how you end your trip, you will have enjoyed your own desert solitaire.

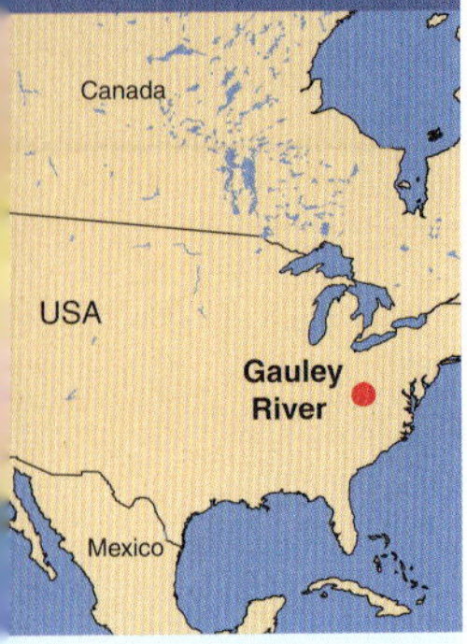


# GAULEY RIVER, VIRGINIA, USA

## Good Gauley – a whitewater gem

**Grade**
3-5

**Experience**
Expert

**Getting there**
The largest airport is at Charleston, 65 miles (105km) from Summersville. If driving, the main entrance to Gauley River National Recreation Area is off U.S. Route 19 south of Summersville and north of Fayetteville (turn onto WV Route 129 toward Summersville Dam). Take the second left after you cross the dam and follow the signs

**In this location**
The rest of the state is also full of classic Class 3-4/5 rivers. Take a road trip and hit Big Sandy Creek, the Cheat River, the Cranberry River, Laurel Fork, Upper and Middle Meadow, and the New River

**On land**
Cool off with a visit to Summersville Lake, visit Carnifex Ferry Battlefield State Park, or take a sampling tour of the nearby Kirkwood Winery

While West Virginia's Gauley River courses 105 miles (169km) through the Appalachian Mountains, merging with the New River to form the Kanawha River, which finally empties into the Ohio, it's a 20-mile (32km) stretch of whitewater below the Summersville Dam in Nicholas County that's one of the best, most concentrated whitewater runs in the country, drawing paddlers from far and wide.

The chief feature of the Gauley River National Recreation Area, the two stretches – the Upper and Lower – are run year-round by recreational boaters and from spring to autumn by commercial outfitters, rainfall permitting. However the real season is called Gauley Season. It starts the Friday after Labor Day (first Monday in September) when the Army Corps of Engineers begins a series of 22 controlled, 2,400–2,800 cubic feet (68-80m$^3$) water releases on six successive four-day weekends (Friday – Monday), specifically for paddlers. The water owes itself to the first law passed in the United States mandating recreational whitewater releases.

The whitewater sections include the 9.8-mile (15.8km), Class 4-5 Upper and the slightly easier Class 3-4 Lower, which are connected with a 5.5-mile (8.8km) middle section. With a take-out for the Upper and put-in for the Lower at Woods Ferry, public access is easy.

After marvelling at the flumes of water jetting out of the dam, you'll get a taste of the Upper section's whitewater right away. Shortly after the put-in come such rapids as not-so-aptly named Insignificant and Pillow Rock, which seasoned kayakers sometimes try to splat into a rocket move. It was near here where the American Civil War's Battle of Carnifex Ferry took place on 10 September 1861, resulting in a Union victory.

You'll have your own war to continue waging against the river's whitewater, however, as next up come the four drops of Lost Paddle Rapid, Iron Ring and Sweet's Falls, named for Gauley pioneer John Sweet. All in all, it's as full a day of continuous whitewater as you'll find anywhere.

The rapids on the Lower section are slightly easier and more spread out, but still world class. Included are such named cascades as Wood's Ferry, marked by a series of pour-overs, as well as PJ's Hole and Julie's Juicer; Koontz's Flume, recognised by an enormous undercut; Canyon Doors; the boulder gardens of Upper and Lower Mash; and good ol' Rocky Top. The run finishes out with the wave trains of Heaven's Gate, Upper and Lower Staircase and Rollercoaster, giving you two great sections of whitewater over the same weekend.

If you're into the party scene as much as paddling, hit the river during Gauley Fest weekend, the largest annual fundraiser for river conservation organisation American Whitewater. A watery version of Woodstock, it's held every third weekend in September, drawing paddlers from the across the country for a weekend of camping, debauchery, bands, booths, mud and plenty of paddling.

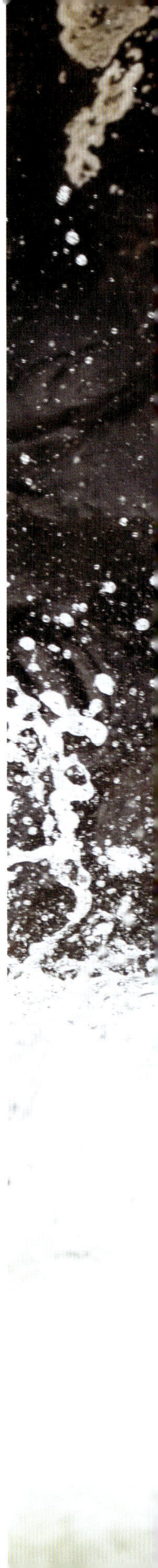

SEA KAYAKING

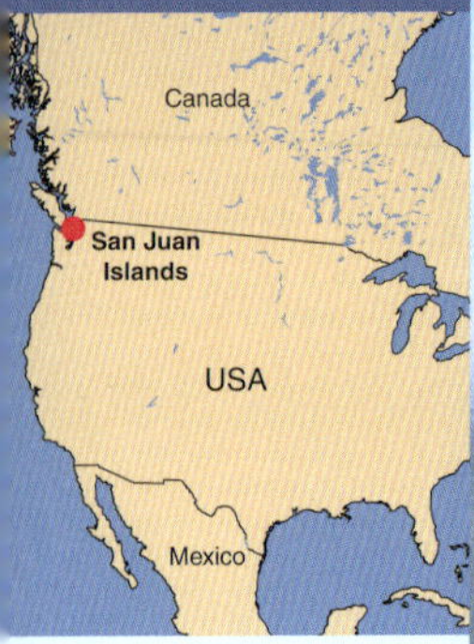


**Experience**
Novice

**Getting there**
From Seattle, take the train, bus or hire a car to Anacortes to catch a ferry to the islands. Or fly from Seattle-Tacoma airport (weekdays only). On arrival (and with a reservation), San Juan Transit can pick you up from Friday Harbor and take you to your launch point

**In this location**
To explore a different island, try Eastsound on Orcas Island, it's less populated than Friday Harbor and offers great day trips to surrounding islands from North Beach

**On land**
Take a bottle of local wine and a picnic to San Juan County Park to raise your flutes to whale flukes at sunset. Another hotspot for whales is Johnstone Strait in British Columbia. Located in sheltered waters away from the reserve, Johnstone is considered one of the best places in the world to watch orcas

# SAN JUAN ISLANDS, WASHINGTON, USA

## An oasis for sea kayakers and orcas alike

To paddle with whales, it doesn't get any better than Washington's San Juan Islands. And seeing them is no fluke; the nutrient-rich waters of nearby Haro Strait lure them back to their feeding grounds every year.

The most popular place to base your trip is to ferry to Friday Harbor on San Juan Island. There you can tool around various bays and islands and eventually make your way out into the orca zone of Haro Strait. Hit it during the summer and you're almost guaranteed to encounter these black and white behemoths.

Three pods totalling about 84 orcas forage through the boundary water straits throughout the summer, relying on its food-laden waters to sustain their migrations. For the best chance of sighting them, launch from Snug Harbor in Mitchell Bay. Many paddlers also wait until they see them from a vantage point on shore before heading out.

To get to their main feeding grounds, head east from Mitchell Bay and bear south along the coast toward Deadman's Cove, about an hour's paddle, depending on the tide direction. Most of the shoreline

is private beach or cliffside, but you can rest at various pull-outs en route. About halfway there you'll pass Smallpox Bay and San Juan County Park, where public restrooms, a picnic area and a soft drink vending machine are available. For shorter paddles, the park also offers a place to park your car to end your tour.

Once you see the whales, make sure you don't get too close. The Marine Mammal Protection Act (MMPA) requires boaters to avoid approaches closer than 100 feet (30m) of all whales. And don't have your blinders on to other marine life. The area also teems with Dall's porpoise, river otter and harbour seals.

Another great paddling option is to head to quaint Roche Harbor on the opposite end of the island from bustling Friday Harbor and tour into Pearl Bay around McCracken Point to the north-west side of Henry Island. En route you'll pass an inter-tidal zone with fields of gently swaying eel grass, the 'nursery of the San Juans'; scoop up and pop dead man's fingers (fun fact: you can turn the seaweed pods into squirt guns); and coat your skin with rockweed, which acts as a sunscreen.

You'll also see everything from sea stars and lion's mane jellyfish to eagles and great blue herons launching from towering Sitka spruce. Rounding Posey Island, at high tide the smallest state park in the country with a lone campsite atop a rocky bluff, you'll then come to fields of kelp holding fast in the four-knot (7.4kph) current ripping between San Juan and Battleship islands (one of the fastest-growing organisms in the world, kelp can grow up to two feet [0.6m] a day). You'll likely see seals also, lounging on rock outcroppings poking out of Haro Strait.

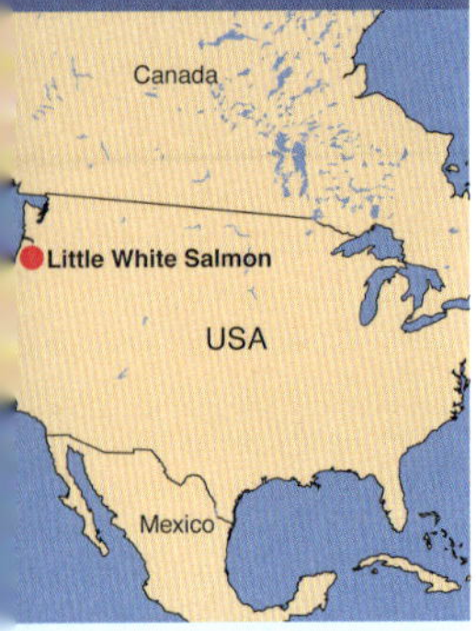


# LITTLE WHITE SALMON, WASHINGTON, USA

## Communing with the spirits on the Little White

**Grade**
5+

**Experience**
Expert

**Getting there**
The Little White is close to the Lewis & Clark Highway on the Washington State side of the Columbia River. Hood River is the nearest town and located at Exit 63 on Interstate 84. It is approximately 60 miles (96km) east of Portland, where the nearest international airport is situated

**In this location**
Both Washington and Oregon have some world-class whitewater rivers. Standouts include the Green Truss section of the White Salmon, Canyon Creek and the Deschutes River

**On land**
Hood River is a hub for all things outdoors and in the summer the hills and mountains provide awesome scope for hiking, mountain biking and climbing. The Columbia River Gorge is a hot-bed for windsurfing and kite surfing enthusiasts

From the moment you put in there is no let up in the gradient and severity of the Little White Salmon. For a little river its reputation is BIG. If you have the nerve, experience and skill, it'll reward you with an exhilarating adventure. It begins as a tough, technical, continuous boulder problem, before the gradient steepens and the whole river seems to drop off the end of the world. Then, just as you're getting to grips with the relentless nature of the river, the Little White changes in character and the drops start to get bigger, in a series of large waterfalls.

Getting Busy is the first serious rapid and it is long! If this half-mile (0.8km) long boulder garden fills you with terror rather than adrenaline-buzzin' joy, then it may be best to call it a day! If you're feeling the Little White's groove though then buckle up because the ride has just begun. Getting Busy fires you straight in to the nasty Boulder Sluice a tricky drop, with a siphon and undercut ledge and fall. One difficult drop flows straight into another and it's easy for things to start to unravel as the Little White runs away with you until you're at its mercy.

Next comes Island, a drop that surprises the unwary. Below the river begins to change; the boulders subside as it begins to carve a course through the bedrock itself. Inspection from the riverbank is a must as ledges and powerful hydraulics abound and interspersed amongst the relentless rapids, well ... here are the waterfalls!

Sacriledge is the first big fall and has a serious lead in, and a nasty cave below. Double Drop comes next and leads you straight in to S-Turn, a clean 13-foot (4m) drop, followed by a tricky slot. More whitewater carnage, including a very dangerous ledge hole, funnels you straight in to the jaws of Wishbone, an angled 20-foot (6m) waterfall. Next is what many consider to be one of the hardest sections of the river, Stove Pipe. It's a vicious rapid with a deadly, hidden sinkhole, and is usually portaged, but the two smaller drops just upstream hide a monster of their own. A powerful horseshoe-shaped hole sits below the second drop. If you do escape then the river will sweep you into the teeth of Stove Pipe!

Soon you'll reach Spirit Falls, a 35-foot (11m) waterfall. Don't be deceived, Spirit holds some nasty surprises. Get the line wrong and you can find yourself in all kinds of hell.

If you make the line OK, you need to be heading river left like a freight train to avoid Chaos, a horrendous hole that has nearly killed several paddlers.

From here the intensity subsides a little, although the Little White still has a few challenges, until you finally make it out to Drano Lake, mentally and physically exhausted, but feeling very much alive. You've communed with the spirits of the Little White ... and lived to tell the tale.

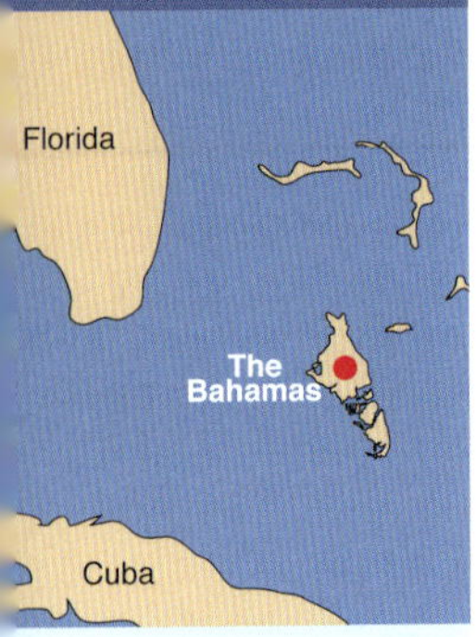


**Experience**
Novice

**Getting there**
The Bahamas are located 100 miles (161km) off the coast of Florida, a few hours by boat or 20 minutes by plane. You can fly direct to Great Exuma Island from Nassau, most major airports in Florida, North Carolina and Atlanta

**In this location**
Head just south of Stocking Island to Mystery Cave, a 400 feet-deep (122m) blue hole that quickly drops to 100 feet (30m). It makes a great day trip from Georgetown

**On land**
Spend time in Georgetown before or after your paddle and take in Government Dock and its restaurant and bar scene. Also, make sure to cross the Tropic of Cancer line, which runs right through town. You can also head to Little Exuma and visit the Hermitage Estate ruins from the cotton plantation days

# BAHAMAS

## Popular with film stars and paddlers alike

You don't have to go all the way to Tahiti for a tropical touring fix. The Bahamas – and especially the Exumas – are a chain of palm-covered islands lined with clear, blue water and white-sand beaches. The 2,500-isle Bahaman archipelago was formed by deposits of shell and coral that now make up one of the world's largest limestone formations. It is such an oasis-like setting for sea kayaking that you may never want to return home.

The Exumas are located well away from the hustle, bustle and tourists of Freeport and Nassau and offer plenty of beaches for camping and pristine water for snorkelling and paddling.

You'll find plenty of solitude as well. Known as the Out Islands, the Exumas, a 120-mile (193km) string of 360 cays, are largely uninhabited, set in water so beautiful that the Bahamian government has protected a 176-square-mile (455km$^2$) section as the Exuma Cays Land and Sea Park. It's the first marine fishery reserve in the Caribbean and one of the world's most successful marine parks, with natural gardens of coral, fish and lobster. The park also harbours stromatolites, a reef-forming algae billed as the oldest living life form on earth.

Most people begin their paddling tours in the town of Georgetown, on Great Exuma, either paddling out from town or hiring a shuttle to go further out into the cays. A short paddle away is a barrier cay protecting the main islands from the Atlantic – stay on the western side to keep out of the wind and swell. You can also climb to a bluff top on Stocking Island for 360-degree views of the area's islands and limestone formations (including a trio of rocks called the Three Sisters).

While many of the cays are private, and home to such stars as Johnny Depp, Tim McGraw and Faith Hill, enough islands and cays are public that you can pull over and camp along the way. For the most part, you'll traverse the leeward side of the Exuma Island chain, paddling from island to island and stopping to snorkel and swim wherever you please. When it comes time to camp, settle in on any number of secluded, palm-lined beaches. It's worth packing a fishing rod so you can barbecue your catch over a campfire. You can also climb down inside blowholes to cool off, visit iguanas on Allen Cay and hike to overlooks to watch the Atlantic's mighty crash into the exposed sides of the islands.

If the weather holds, you can end your trip at Staniel Cay, the hub of the Exuma Cays. Before arriving, make sure to visit Thunderball Cave – as seen in the James Bond movie *Thunderball* and mermaid classic *Splash* – where you can snorkel inside a small cave with thousands of fish. After arriving at Staniel Cay, celebrate with a rum cocktail at the Staniel Cay Yacht Club before hiring a charter plane to fly back to Georgetown.

SEA KAYAKING

**Experience**
Novice

**Getting there**
After flying into Belize City, avoid the long winding road by taking a puddle-jumper flight straight to Dangriga

**In this location**
To get further off the beaten path, head to Halfmoon Cay in the heart of Lighthouse Reef National Park, the first protected marine area in the Caribbean, where you can paddle and sail to the Great Blue Hole, a 400-feet-deep (122m), 1,000-feet-wide (305m) sinkhole

**On land**
Take a day or two on the mainland to visit ancient Mayan Ruins and tour such caves as Actun Tunichil Muknal (ATA), complete with mummies and pottery

# BELIZE

## The second longest barrier reef in the world

If you want to snorkel from your sea kayak, it doesn't get any better than Belize, home to the second largest barrier reef in the world. Here you can island hop to your heart's content, pulling over to snorkel wherever you fancy and turning in each night to a hammock swinging between palm trees.

Considered one of the richest marine ecosystems on the planet, the 185-mile (298km) long Belize Barrier Reef runs from 10 to 25 miles (16-40km) offshore and is the largest reef in the northern hemisphere, second in the world only to Australia's Great Barrier. Strewn along it are more than 225 cays, ranging from small beach and palm-lined islands perched along the reef's edge to larger mangrove islands harbouring snaking passageways.

Teeming with brilliantly coloured fish, coral and sea grass beds, its southern regions are best for sea kayaking, offering one of the most pristine marine ecosystems on the planet.

Start your trip out of the southern coastal community of Dangriga, where you can rent boats and even

camping equipment from Island Expeditions. From there you can motor 36 miles (58km) out to their base camp at Southwest Cays in one of the reef's most spectacular atolls – Glover's Reef, named after pirate John Glover who used the area's islands and reefs as a base from which to raid Spanish merchant ships – or venture on your own to your own remote islets in the atoll.

Declared a marine park in 1993 and World Heritage Site in 1996, Glover's is one of three atolls offshore of Belize and measures roughly 20 miles (32km) long by 7 miles (11km) wide, offering days of exploration. Oval-shaped reef walls climb from the ocean floor and surround a central lagoon with more than 700 patch reefs to explore.

And just a mile (1.6km) off the atoll's eastern shore the reef wall drops 2,600 feet (792m) to the ocean floor. The interaction between the deep, open waters of the Caribbean and the atoll's sheltered lagoons creates a potpourri of marine life perfect for sea kayaking and snorkelling. Simply drop anchor and hop overboard to see what lurks below, or trail your kayak behind you as you snorkel among queen angels, barracuda, nurse sharks, gobi fish, damsels, manta rays, sea turtles, octopus and more.

When it comes time to turn in, you can either stay at B&Bs along the way or camp, all the while paddling through a veritable tropical oasis. You can also take a break from paddling to scuba dive with any number of outfitters strewn throughout the islands.

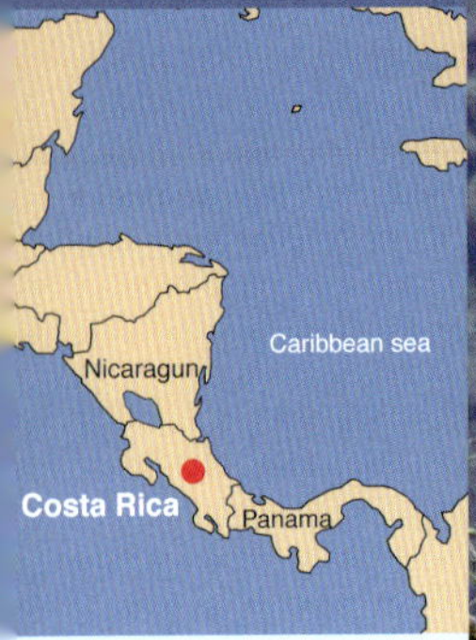


**Experience**
Intermediate – Expert

**Getting there**
Fly into San Jose and plan your trip from there by either renting a car, hiring a driver or flying to the Nicoya or Osa peninsulas. For Osa, most people fly into Puerto Jiménez

**In this location**
Take a break from sea kayaking and try your hand at surfing. Near Manuel Antonio are such world-class breaks as Jaco; the entire Nicoya coast offers great swell (try Tamarindo); and the Osa is also known for its great waves (without the people)

**On land**
Take time out to hike the Parks you parallel by kayak, from Corcovado to Manuel Antonio. Also, try a canopy tour, which will put you eye to eye with creatures you never knew existed

# COSTA RICA

## Touring like a Tico

With 635 miles (1,022km) of shoreline along the Pacific coast and 132 miles (212km) on the Caribbean, and hundred of rivers winding their way inland through tropical jungle, there's no shortage of sea kayaking options in Costa Rica. And most of it is as pristine as paddling gets – the country has the best-developed conservation programme in the world, with 27 percent of its lands protected and 11 percent included in its National Park system.

On the Caribbean side, many tourers head for the inland canals and waterways of the country's north-east corner, which wind inland from the coast to the interior. Overnight options abound at jungle lodges. One good bet is to base out of the coastal town of Tortuguero, where you can explore the coast and inlets and, with a National Park ranger, visit the nesting sea turtle grounds of Tortuguero National Park (best time: full moon during the July – September nesting season).

Even more options exist on the Pacific side. Named for a Conquistador now buried there, 53 miles (85km) from San Jose is 50-year-old Manuel Antonio National Park, where you can paddle in crystal clear waters along white sand beaches lined by an evergreen littoral forest and dense tropical jungle (it,

too, offers the chance to view endangered sea turtles).

As for its wilderness, consider this testimonial from David Rains Wallace, author of *The Quetzal and the Macaw*: 'On a short trail leading from the beaches, three-toed sloths were visible every few hundred feet, draped like soiled scatter-rugs over Cecropia trees, while troops of squirrel monkeys fed busily on swarms of green and black grasshoppers ...' If you do go, bring raingear; the Park receives 151 inches (384cm) of precipitation a year (January and February are the driest months).

Further north is the Nicoya Peninsula, which harbours a dozen or so unoccupied islands off its coast for island-hopping, paddling and camping. Access it by ferrying from Puntarenas to Playa Naranjo and then follow the coast south from island to island down to Paquera. Fed by the Tempisque River, its gulf is home to dolphin, frigate birds, porpoise, sea turtles, orcas and more (including plenty of fish to barbecue over the campfire).

In the country's southern end, try the Osa Peninsula, billed as the most biologically diverse place on earth. Drake Bay's micro-climate in the rain shadow of the Talamanca Mountains means no wind until noon, meaning calm early morning paddles. Paddle throughout the bay and its many inlets, or tour the Pacific coastline from Carate north up toward Corcovado National Park. While the area's surf can make the coastal paddling a bit rough, two lagoons in Carate offer great calm water touring amongst caymans, crocodiles and such wading birds as herons, egrets and ibis. When you're through paddling, tour the Park with a local naturalist or snorkel the seamounts of Cano National Park.

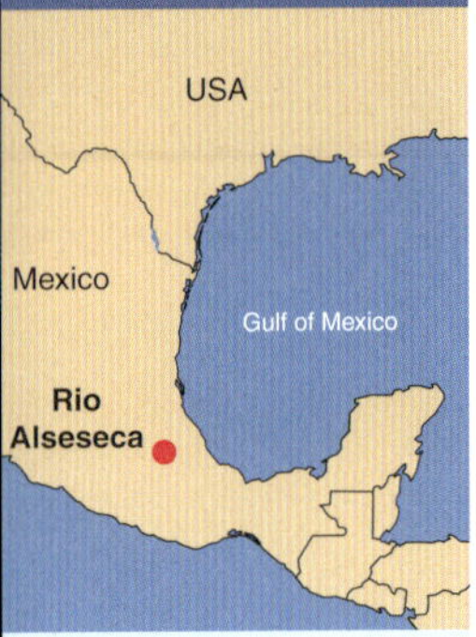


**Grade**
4-5

**Experience**
Expert

**Getting there**
Fly to Mexico City or Veracruz and then head towards Tlapacoyan

**In this location**
Veracruz State is full of whitewater gems; ask at a local rafting company for tips and water levels

**On land**
Mexico is full of friendly people and exciting things to see and do, just go out and explore

# RIO ALSESECA, MEXICO

## One of the best single-river kayaking destinations

Veracruz State in Mexico is home to many fine whitewater rivers, but the Rio Alseseca stands out as one of the steepest and most challenging for whitewater kayakers. Even the easiest roadside section is only easy when compared to the rest of the river. Countless small waterfalls and slides follow each other in quick succession as water races over the hard bedrock. The hardest rapid on this section is the S-turn where the whole river thunders over a 90-degree twisting waterfall into a narrow mini-canyon. For those paddlers brave enough to attempt it, it will be a ride of your life!

Further upstream from the roadside section there is also a short section of slightly harder rapids including Vaseline, a slot drop so narrow that you can almost not believe there is enough room for your kayak to pass through without getting stuck. Sitting above the slot trying to eyeball your line sets your pulse racing, the slide into Boof Combo after the narrow slot is tricky too. The adrenaline races through your veins as you take your last strokes and tuck up to fit through the slot, just as you want to celebrate not getting stuck your kayak accelerates towards a horizon line, one well-timed stroke and Whoosh! you are flying through the air into a big pool of calm water.

The biggest waterfall on the Rio Alseseca is Big Banana; it was first successfully attempted in 2010 by two brave paddlers. At just under 131 feet (40m) it is one of the biggest waterfalls ever descended in a kayak! It takes a huge amount of training, planning and confidence to attempt such a massive waterfall, years of jumping smaller waterfalls and practising the correct take-off and landing techniques. A strong team to back you up in the event of an accident is, of course, a necessity. However, the most important quality any paddler who wishes to attempt such an extreme stunt needs is the ability to make decisions quickly and calmly, deciding whether to go or not to go, and then keeping a clear head as you approach the lip of the biggest waterfall of your life, timing the last stroke to perfection then tucking up as you fall, fall, fall down into the chaotic, boiling water in the plunge pool, orientating yourself underwater then eskimo rolling your kayak back up. Only the very best paddlers in the world have the skills to attempt such a waterfall and even they will need a dose of luck to ensure a safe descent!

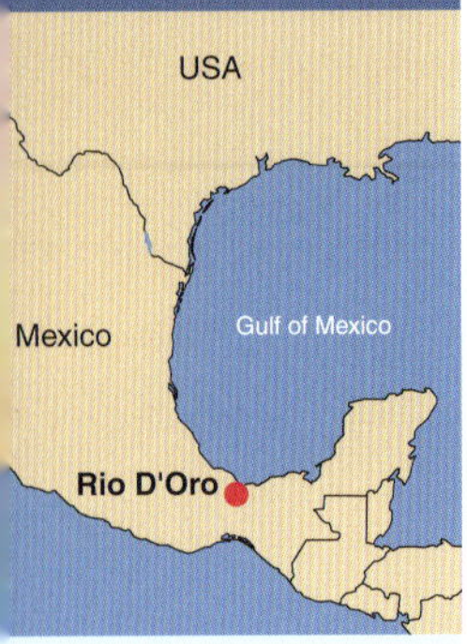


**Grade**
4-5

**Experience**
Expert

**Getting there**
Fly to Mexico City then connect to Veracruz, rent a 4X4, buy a map and head south along the coast until you reach Costa de Oro where the Rio de Oro flows into the ocean

**In this location**
Veracruz State has loads of awesome whitewater including the Alsesca and the Fliobobos

**On land**
Mexican culture is vibrant and the people very friendly, an inquisitive traveller will find something of interest at every turn

# RIO DE ORO, MEXICO

## Jungle paddling paradise

The Rio de Oro in Veracruz State, Mexico is without doubt one of the most amazing day's paddling that Mexico has to offer. The Oro has all the ingredients for an ultimate day on the river. There are two ways to reach the put-in, choose either a two to three hour hike over farmland or engage in a bit of bargaining with the local farmers and drive as far as your vehicle can before hiking the rest of the way. The put-in is near an orange orchard just below a huge waterfall and surrounded by luscious green vegetation and trees, giving it a real jungle adventure feeling.

The clear warm water weaves its way through boulder gardens and over small step drops, providing a short warm up before closing in and entering the smaller of the two gorges. Fast flowing rapids and drop-offs challenge the paddler to find and keep their line as the Oro blasts through the narrow rock gorge, winding its way deeper into the jungle-like surroundings. A narrowing of the river and a horizon line signals the start of the second gorge and the real action.

The entrance to the second gorge is guarded by a 40 feet (12m) waterfall and is certainly not for the faint hearted! The narrow shoot of water drops and twists into a big pool below and, once you are in, there is no way out except to carry on. For the less adventurous it is possible to get out on the river right-hand side and walk around the second gorge and put in again below it. Several short, but technically challenging rapids are hidden in the gorge before it becomes wider and presents another horizon line, the second exit, waterfall. The second waterfall is slightly smaller, 30 feet (9m), and technically easier than the first, but should not be underestimated, it is still a pretty big jump in a canoe.

The last section of the Oro is the easiest and most exciting; from the second waterfall the river flows through easy rapids all the way into the ocean! The Rio de Oro is the only river I know of that starts with a hike into the jungle, provides stunning, technically challenging whitewater, two big waterfalls and then easy rapids all the way to the beach. When you reach the ocean turn left and paddle along the beach until you reach a beach shack restaurant where you can order cold beer and freshly cooked prawns, and then sleep on the beach; life does not get any better.

liquidlogic

**Experience**
Novice

**Getting there**
You can take direct flights to either Cabo San Lucas or straight into La Paz. You can fly to Loreto from both airports as well as Los Angeles

**In this location**
If you tire of your sea kayak, take to the Sea of Cortez on a stand up paddleboard, which perches you far enough above its aquamarine water to see even more marine life

**On land**
Ever tried kite boarding? Now's your chance. Just south of La Paz is the kite boarding Mecca of La Ventana, where you can rent boards and take lessons. In Loreto, visit the town's mission church and historical museum

# SEA OF CORTEZ, MEXICO

## Paddle with sea lions

Named after Spanish pirate and explorer Hernan Cortez – who sought jewels and other riches for his crown back home – the sparkling Sea of Cortez is a crown jewel for sea kayaking.

Located on the east side of Mexico's Baja Peninsula, its waters follow a jagged coastline chock full of islands, bays and beaches for exploring. The region is also rich in marine life, letting you tour alongside seals, sea lions, dolphins and whales – and enjoy fresh fish on the grill every night. Plant life on shore is equally diverse, from towering, sentry-like barrel cactus to forests of cardons.

Due to the protection of the mountains, the water is much calmer than the nearby Pacific, with the wake of your kayak often the only ripple in sight. Still, don't discount the winds. In December and January, El Nortes can howl southward from the States, creating dangerous conditions. Most paddlers make their miles in the morning and adopt the popular siesta pastime in the afternoons (no matter what month you go, avoid long crossings, especially in the afternoon).

Two of the most popular areas for sea kayaking are near La Paz and Loreto. To sea kayak with sea lions, head to La Paz, where a three-mile (5km) crossing takes you to the north end of Espiritu Santo island and its famous sea lion rookery. Famed for its role in John Steinbeck's *The Pearl,* Espiritu Santo is actually one large island surrounded by five neighbours, all renowned for their rugged landscape, aquamarine water, white beaches and convoluted coastlines. The island's western side is especially appealing with easily accessible beaches, twisting canyons and a variety of plant and animal life (keep your eyes peeled for the ring-tailed cat).

But the stars of the show are the sea lions. The best place to see, paddle and (if you dare) swim with them is a small chain of islets just north of the main island where they bask in the Baja sun. To get there, most private boaters launch from Puerto Balandra or Playa el Tecolote just north of La Paz.

North of La Paz, Loreto's Gulf islands, recently designated a National Marine Park, have been called Mexico's Galapagos for their plant and animal life. Countless islands are yours to explore, including Coronado, Danzante, Monserrate and Carmen where you can steer your rudder toward hidden bays, arches and sea caves. Turn your head skyward and you can marvel at blue-footed boobies, frigate birds and brown pelicans.

For an extended tour, tackle the 150-mile (241km) stretch from Loreto to La Paz, following the remote Sierra de la Giganta Mountains past expansive cliffs, sea stacks and arches. Just get most of your miles in early, dodging the wind, while leaving plenty of time for snorkelling, siestas and sunset happy hours in the afternoon.

**Grade**
4-5

**Experience**
Expert

**Getting there**
The Rio Manso is in the Río Negro Province of Argentina near to the Chilean border. Whatever method of transport you choose it will be a long mission to get there

**In this location**
Right next door to the Duckslide is the Cascada del los Alerces, another superb waterfall for expert whitewater kayakers to test their mettle on. The rest of the Manso gorge below the two falls is tricky with plenty of challenging rapids

**On land**
The Argentinean side of the Andes is an incredibly beautiful corner of the world, hiking, chilling by one of the many lakes, fishing or taking a bus tour, and of course eating steak washed down with red wine

# MANSO RIVER, ARGENTINA

## Look before you leap

Duckslide is one of two classic Alerces waterfalls on the Rio Manso in Argentina. After a beautiful flat water cruise the river splits in two and roars over a pair of superb waterfalls for expert whitewater kayakers.

Surrounded by the beautiful Andes mountains, floating along the calm and tranquil Rio Manso, it is easy to forget the mission of the day, hucking waterfalls. The contrast couldn't be more extreme, a river so flat and calm it mirrors the amazing mountain landscape that rises up from the shore to the clouds, then suddenly forks in two and drops over 40 feet (12m) into a big pool and the start of the Manso gorge.

Scouting the Duckslide reveals an easy line, paddle towards the middle of the lip, slide the slide and tuck on entry. If paddling waterfalls was really that easy then everybody would be doing them! Scrambling around on the slippery rock above the slide allows for a good view of the line, checking every foot to be sure there are no random jets of water that could push the kayak off line or, even worse, capsize it. A crash landing from 40 feet (12m) could cause a serious injury and a serious injury at the bottom of a waterfall in the Andes mountains is the type of incident that could turn into an epic.

Too long spent scouting the line can lead to excess worry or nerves, so the key is to spend long enough to gain sufficient information to run the line safely, but not too long, with the line planned and saved into your head, safety and camera set, then all that is left to do is strap in and huck the meat! Sliding into your kayak, wriggling your feet and hips into place is all part of the routine; pop on the spray deck and check the lip is correctly fitted. Grab hold of your paddle and test the grip, circling your shoulders and neck to warm up the muscles in preparation for a hard landing, go through the line one last time in your head, ready.

A clenched fist on top of your helmet is a universal signal in the whitewater world for OK, everybody is ready: three, two, one, GO! Powerful paddle strokes out of the staging eddy propel the kayak towards the lip, the drop looks huge, there's no turning back, your pulse is pounding. The sound of the rushing water is all encompassing, the brief view from the lip towards the landing zone is incredible, the last corrective strokes to optimise the line, falling, sliding, a last glimpse to focus on the landing, tuck your head down forwards and tuck your paddle into the side of the kayak to charge into the boiling water at the bottom of the fall. The force of the landing is hard, hold your position and wait until the water frees you. A lucky line will resurface you – head up and looking good, then feelings of relief and ecstasy flow through your nervous system, wow.

**Experience**
Intermediate – Expert

**Getting there**
Your best bet is to fly to Puerto Montt (catch a connector flight from Santiago) and work out ground and/or water transportation from there to Puerto Varas and/or Hornopirén

**In this location**
The island of Chiloé, just west off the mainland of Continental Chile, is also a prime paddling hotspot, steeped in Chilean culture

**On land**
Take some time to explore Pumalin Park, a nature reserve created by environmentalist Douglas Tompkins. From sea to the top of towering peaks, it's designed to protect an entire bio-region

# LAKE DISTRICT, CHILE

## Sea kayaking and hot springs

If you have the time, ability and penchant for soaking in hot springs after the day's paddle, head to Puerto Varas, Chile, to kayak the fjords of the Chilean Lake district.

Chile's fjordlands harbour everything you could want in a sea kayak trip, from lush Alerce forests – including what's rumoured to be the oldest tree in the world at 4,500 years – and intricate coastlines, to chains of islands, glaciers, colourful culture and hot springs to soothe sore muscles after each day's paddle. Wildlife also abounds in the region. On the water you're likely to paddle among sea lions, orcas and austral dolphins. Cast your eyes skyward and you'll likely see petrels, albatrosses and cormorants flying overhead against the backdrop of the Andes. If your wildlife stars are aligned, you might even see parrots flying over penguins, further illustrating the region's bio-diversity.

This sea kayaking tour through Comau Fjord, located on the east side of the Huequi Peninsula on the

country's west coast, begins in the hamlet of Hornopirén. Many people opt to camp at Quintupeu Fjord – known as the hiding place of the German battleship *Dresden* during the Battle of the Falkland Islands in 1914 – which starts near the tip of Llancahue Island. Or you can book lodging and a home-cooked meal on site. At the southern part of Quintupeu lies the mouth of Comau Fjord, which narrows to a width of less than one mile (1.6km). In its reach are beaches and cascading waterfalls that plunge straight into the ocean. After paddling among sea lion colonies and marvelling at the fjord's granite slopes dropping straight into the water, you can soak in the pools of the Llancahue Hot Springs, located on the island of the same name. A good campsite is located up near the hot springs, where the Pumalin Park facilities can be used by visitors.

Further south is the settlement of Huinay along the Huinay River. After this day's paddle, you can relax in the Porcelana hot springs on the Huequi Peninsula along the Porcelana River. The final stretch takes you to Leptepú, where you can portage to Largo Fjord before continuing on to Reñihué Fjord. Depending on time, you can finish with a tour of Pumalin Park, a 1,250-square-mile (3,240km$^2$) nature reserve created by environmentalist Douglas Tompkins, and soak in the Cahuelmó hot springs at the end of the Cahuelmo Fjord before ferrying back to Puerto Montt.

**Grade**
4-5

**Experience**
Intermediate – Expert

**Getting there**
Getting to the Futa is an adventure in itself. Many intrepid paddlers choose to buy or rent a car and drive. Other options include flying into Puerto Montt in Chile and taking a smaller flight or bus from there

**In this location**
Several rivers in the region can be enjoyed as a warm up for the Futa or just a change of pace. The Rio Azul flows into the Futa and the Rio Neltume, Fuy and San Pedro are a few hours' drive away

**On land**
The Futaleufú National Park in Patagonia is one of the most beautiful places in the world, with blue-green water, lush vegetation and snow-capped mountains for hiking, fly fishing and taking in the vista

# FUTALEUFÚ RIVER, CHILE

## Whitewater bonanza

The Futaleufú is regarded by many professional whitewater paddlers as one of the best rivers in the world. With its huge rapids and waves, breathtaking scenery, the Futa will be an adventure you will never forget.

Its name says it all: Inferno Canyon. This is the uppermost whitewater section of Chile's Futaleufú River, and if you're not careful it lives up to its billing.

Reaching the Gates of Inferno will get every paddler's adrenaline pumping; steep rock walls close in from both sides, funnelling the entire might of the river into steep, boiling Class 4-5 rapids. Massive hydraulics and diagonals pulse and explode in every direction; the noise of the crashing water is everywhere. The key is to stay calm and paddle furiously to stay on line as you battle through the chasm's successive rapids.

That's not to say there isn't some sanctuary to be found. Between the biggest rapids are long pools of gently flowing water where you can recover, relax and prepare for the next whitewater onslaught.

But don't let your game down for too long. Below Inferno Canyon is one of the most famous rapids on the Futa, the Throne Room. The Throne Room is even bigger and steeper than it looks from the shore, its waves rising up like the surrounding Andes. The plan is simple: slalom around the big breaking waves at the top and then turn and surf the wave formed by the massive Throne Rock in the middle, building up speed to shoot left at the bottom to avoid a big, evil-looking wave. Two things are key: don't forget where you are and try not to end up in the big whirlpool behind Throne Rock, or the aptly named Toaster eddy to the right.

Further downstream is the Terminator section, one of the most complete sections of whitewater anywhere in the world, with big volume, technical lines and surf waves all set in deep turquoise-blue water and jaw-dropping surroundings. The section has hard lines and easy lines; hard is down the gut, and easy is far left. Of course, easy is all relative, still requiring Class 4 skills. Hint: Take a deep breath before venturing out into the middle to try to surf the Terminator wave; trying to stay in control in its huge foam pile while bouncing crazily on its fast, green ramp of water is no easy feat.

Just like Arnold Schwarzenegger comes back in his Hollywood blockbusters, the river comes back as well, with yet another classic whitewater stretch immediately below: the Bridge to Bridge section. With countless waves to surf and mountainous wave trains, this section offers some of the best big water kayaking on the planet.

Mundaka is regarded by many Futa guides as the best rapid on the river, a huge, chaotic, boiling mess of water thundering downstream ending in a huge breaking wave that flips even the biggest rafts. And below lie such classics as Tiburon (Hint: try to catch the surf wave at top), Mas o Menos and Casa de Piedras.

**Grade**
3-6

**Experience**
Intermediate – Expert

**Getting there**
After flying to Quito it's about a six-hour drive to the Quijos valley (get to it by driving down the Avenue of the Volcanoes through town)

**In this location**
While the area teems with whitewater, work it out ahead of time and you can also plan a sea kayaking excursion to the Galapagos

**On land**
Spend some time in Quito, the ancient Incan and modern capital of Ecuador, to explore its many museums and plan side trips to 19,614-foot (5,978m) Cotopaxi, the highest active volcano in the world, and a shopping spree at the famous Otavalo market

# ECUADOR

## Ecuadorian ecstasy – seven rivers in as many days

Kayak in Ecuador and you'll follow torrent ducks-off horizon lines, plan moves around blue morpho butterflies and have your shoulders so sore by week's end that you'll have trouble reaching the overhead on the flight home.

To get to this whitewater wonderland, most kayakers head out of Quito over the 13,460-foot (4,103m) Papallacta Pass before descending 8,000 feet (2,438m) into the Amazon Basin and town of Baeza. It's the same route that Gonzalo Pizarro and Francisco de Orellana took 500 years earlier in their ill-fated search for El Dorado, which led to the discovery of the Amazon.

But you'll be discovering whitewater. 15 miles (24km) and 13,000 vertical feet (3,962m) away is the 18,866-foot (5,750m) peak of the Antisana volcano, providing the gradient that funnels the valley's 70 inches (178cm) of rain per year down dozens of jungle tributaries, all feeding the Rio Quijos. The result is a haven for Class 3-4 boaters, letting you paddle a different run every day of the week. Within an hour of the riverside Small World Adventures Lodge – which marks the put-in for one world-class run, and the take-out for two others – are 14 different Class 3 or higher runs on five different rivers, with another dozen toward Tena.

The runs include everything from cloud forest creeks and creek / playboat combos to huge volume rivers with big water play. Sometimes you'll find everything all on the same run. You can either bring your own boat or rent one from Small World, which claims to carry 'the world's largest kayak fleet in Ecuador'.

Classics to hit during the season from November to April include the Quijos, which has several Class 3-4 runs, and a hair-raising Class 5-6 in its upper reaches. Another classic is the Rio Oyacachi, a Class-4 maze filled with horizon lines that eventually dumps into the Quijos. To refuel and rest, head into one of several small villages and dine on fresh empanadas, fruit plates and llapin gacho, a potato pancake with cheese that's a local specialty.

Tire of the Quijos valley and you can drive over an 8,000-foot (2,438m) pass into Tena to hit the Upper and Lower Misahuallí, and Upper Jondachi, all with rounded boulders, clear water, fern-lined walls and volcano-sized gradient. While the Misahuallí has been likened to 'the Gauley, with parrots', put the Upper Jondachi on your list too. Its 85 Class 3-5 rapids are outnumbered only by its parrots and butterflies and you'll run it Blue-Angel-style, catching an eddy, watching your partner disappear, and then following suit before the next person takes your place in line. Cap off the week in the Papallacta Hotsprings, where the conquistadores soaked their bones five centuries ago.

# PHOTO CREDITS

**Europe**

| | | |
|---|---|---|
| 7 | River Danube, Europe | © Angus Gormley / Shutterstock.com |
| 9 | Allier Gorge, France | © Rob Estivill |
| 11 | River Guil, France | © Stephanie CROCQ / Shutterstock.com |
| 13 | Rizzanese River, Corsica | © Jason Smith |
| 15 | Verdon Grand Canyon, France | © Deb Pinniger |
| 17 | Crete, Greece | © www.seakayakgreece.com |
| 19 | Annamoe & Glenmacnass Rivers, Ireland | © Jason Smith |
| 21 | Irish Coast | © Frank Luerweg / Dreamstime.com |
| 23 | Amalfi Coats, Italy | © Lucamato / Dreamstime.com |
| 25 | Venice, Italy | © Joachim Pfoertner / iStock |
| 27 | Ticino River, Italy | © Reproduced by permission of James Weir |
| 29 | Tara River Gorge, Montenegro | © Deb Pinniger |
| 31 | Friesland, The Netherlands | © Mayola Dijksman |
| 33 | Voss & Sjoa, Norway | © Deb Pinniger |
| 35 | Masurian Lake District, Poland | © Puchan / Dreamstime.com |
| 37 | Lake Baikal, Russia | © kav38/ Shutterstock.com |
| 39 | Soča River, Slovenia | © Reproduced by permission of James Weir |
| 41 | Bakio, Spain | © Steve Childs |
| 43 | Costa Brava, Spain | © Francisco Javier Sureda / Dreamstime.com |
| 45 | Mallorca, Spain | © Lucinda Manouch |
| 47 | Mundaka, Spain | © Nathan Eades |
| 49 | Santa Pola, Spain | © KDF Fotografia |
| 51 | Kungsleden, Sweden | © Rob Estivill |
| 53 | Sankt Anna Archipelago, Sweden | © Caroline Dawson |
| 55 | Tessin, Switzerland | © Reproduced by permission of James Weir<br>Photograph by Susanne Spölmink |
| 57 | Vorderrhein River, Switzerland | © Reproduced by permission of James Weir<br>Photograph by Susanne Spölmink |
| 59 | Wastwater, Lake District, England | © Julian Hodgson / iStock |
| 61 | Devizes to Westminster, England | © Hutchinson |
| 63 | Regent's Canal, London, England | © Chris Scott |
| 65 | Norfolk Broads, England | © Oksana Krasiuk / Dreamstime.com |
| 67 | Lundy Island, England | © Deb Pinniger |
| 69 | River Dart, England | © Jason Smith |
| 71 | Isles of Scilly, England | © Sealand Aerial Photography / FBL |
| 73 | River Tweed, Scotland | © Ross Montandon |
| 75 | Outer Hebrides, Scotland | © versevend / iStock.com |
| 77 | Glen Etive, Scotland | © Josh Wedgwood / Unsplash.com |
| 79 | Falls of Lora, Oban, Scotland | © Deb Pinniger |
| 81 | Loch Ard, Scotland | © Emma Hepplewhite |
| 83 | Anglesey & Holy Island, Wales | © Gail Johnson / Dreamstime.com |
| 85 | Bitches Tidal Race, Wales | © Deb Pinniger |
| 87 | Fairy Glen, Snowdonia, Wales | © Tom Laws |
| 89 | Trefor, Llŷn Peninsula, Wales | © Caroline Dawson |

**Africa & Asia**

| | | |
|---|---|---|
| 91 | The White Nile, Uganda | © Deb Pinniger |
| 93 | Morocco | © Ross Montandon |
| 95 | Seychelles | © Iris Joschko / Dreamstime.com |
| 97 | Orange River, South Africa | © Kevin Gillot / Dreamstime.com |
| 99 | Mana Pools National Park, Zimbabwe | © Catherine Sneyd / Shutterstock.com |
| 101 | Zambezi River, Africa | © Deb Pinniger |
| 103 | Nam Suang & Seng Rivers, Laos | © Rob Estivill |
| 105 | Karnali River, Nepal | © NikeSh / Dreamstime.com |
| 107 | Madi Khola River, Nepal | © Jason Smith |
| 109 | Phang Nga Bay, Thailand | © Kevin Hellon / Shutterstock.com |
| 111 | Hạ Long Bay, Vietnam | © Dong Nhat Huy / Shutterstock.com |

**Australasia & Pacific**

| | | |
|---|---|---|
| 113 | Peron Peninsula & Shark Bay, Australia | © electra / Shutterstock.com |
| 115 | Freycinet National Park, Tasmania, Australia | © Steve Lovegrove / Dreamstime.com |
| 117 | Franklin River, Tasmania, Australia | © Matt Newton / www.matthewnewton.com.au |
| 119 | Fitzroy River, Australia | © Chris Scott |
| 121 | Whitsunday Islands, Australia | © ArtTower / Pixabay |
| 123 | Fiji | © Don Mammoser / Shutterstock.com |
| 125 | Hawai'i | © Melissa Burovac / Shutterstock.com |
| 127 | Abel Tasman National Park, New Zealand | © Irina88w / Dreamstime.com |
| 129 | Great Barrier Island, New Zealand | © Mike Dawson / Shutterstock.com |
| 131 | South Island, New Zealand | © Reproduced by permission of James Weir Photograph by Susanne Spölmink |
| 133 | South-East Pacific | © Rico Leffanta / Dreamstime.com |

**North America**

| | | |
|---|---|---|
| 135 | Bowron Lake National Park, Canada | © John Cousins |
| 137 | Skookumchuck Narrows, Canada | © YiBaoTY / Shutterstock.com |
| 139 | Dipper Creek, Canada | © Dcb Pinniger |
| 141 | Lachine Rapids, Montreal, Canada | © Reproduced by permission of James Weir. Photograph by Michael Schomann |
| 143 | Nahanni National Park, Canada | © All Canada Photos / Alamy |
| 145 | Mountain River, Canada | © Justine Curgenven / CackleTV.com |
| 147 | Algonquin Provincial Park, Canada | © Theotivity / Shutterstock.com |
| 149 | Ottawa River, Canada | © David Bainbridge |
| 151 | Inland Rivers, Greenland | © Simon Tapley, Mike Scutt, Graham Milton and Ali Marshall |
| 153 | Sermiligaaq-Tasiilaq Fjord, Greenland | © Adwo / Dreamstine.com |
| 155 | Kongakut River, Alaska, USA | © Design Pics Inc / Alamy |
| 157 | Glacier Bay National Park, Alaska, USA | © Thomas Lange / Dreamstime.com |
| 159 | Talkeetna River, Alaska, USA | © Patrick E Planer / Shutterstock.com |
| 161 | Grand Canyon, Arizona, USA | © Deb Pinniger |
| 163 | Buffalo River, Arkansas, USA | © Craig Hanson / Dreamstime.com |
| 165 | Big Bend Paddling Trail, Florida, USA | © Florida Fish and Wildlife Conservation Commission |
| 167 | Payette River, Idaho, USA | © Tracy King / Dreamstime.com |
| 169 | St Croix & St John Rivers, Maine, USA | © John Lazenby / Dreamstime.com |
| 171 | Acadia National Park, Maine, USA | © Zhukovsky / Dreamstime.com |
| 173 | Lake Superior, Michigan, USA | © Martin Sliger / Shutterstock.com |
| 175 | Boundary Waters, Minnesota, USA | © Wildnerdpix / Shutterstock.com |
| 177 | Litle White Salmon, North Carolina, USA | © Reproduced by permission of James Weir Photograph by Ted Hayes |
| 179 | Labyrinth & Stillwater Canyons, Utah, USA | © Dave Costello |
| 181 | Gauley River, Virginia, USA | © Wirestock / Dreamstime.com |
| 183 | San Juan Islands, Washington, USA | © Mickem / Dreamstime.com |
| 185 | Little White Salmon, Washington, USA | © James Farquharson |

**Central & South America**

| | | |
|---|---|---|
| 187 | Bahamas | © ksmith0808 / Shutterstock.com |
| 189 | Belize | © Simon Dannhauer / Shutterstock.com |
| 191 | Costa Rica | © Wollertz / Dreamstime.com |
| 193 | Rio Alseseca, Mexico | © Reproduced by permission of James Weir |
| 195 | Rio de Oro, Mexico | © Reproduced by permission of James Weir |
| 197 | Sea of Cortez, Mexico | © Beeqisherman / Dreamstime.com |
| 199 | Manso River, Argentina | © Reproduced by permission of James Weir Photograph by Ron Fischer |
| 201 | Lake District, Chile | © DoraDalton / iStock.com |
| 203 | Futaleufú River, Chile | © Guaxinim / Shutterstock.com |
| 205 | Equador | © Darcy Gaechter |

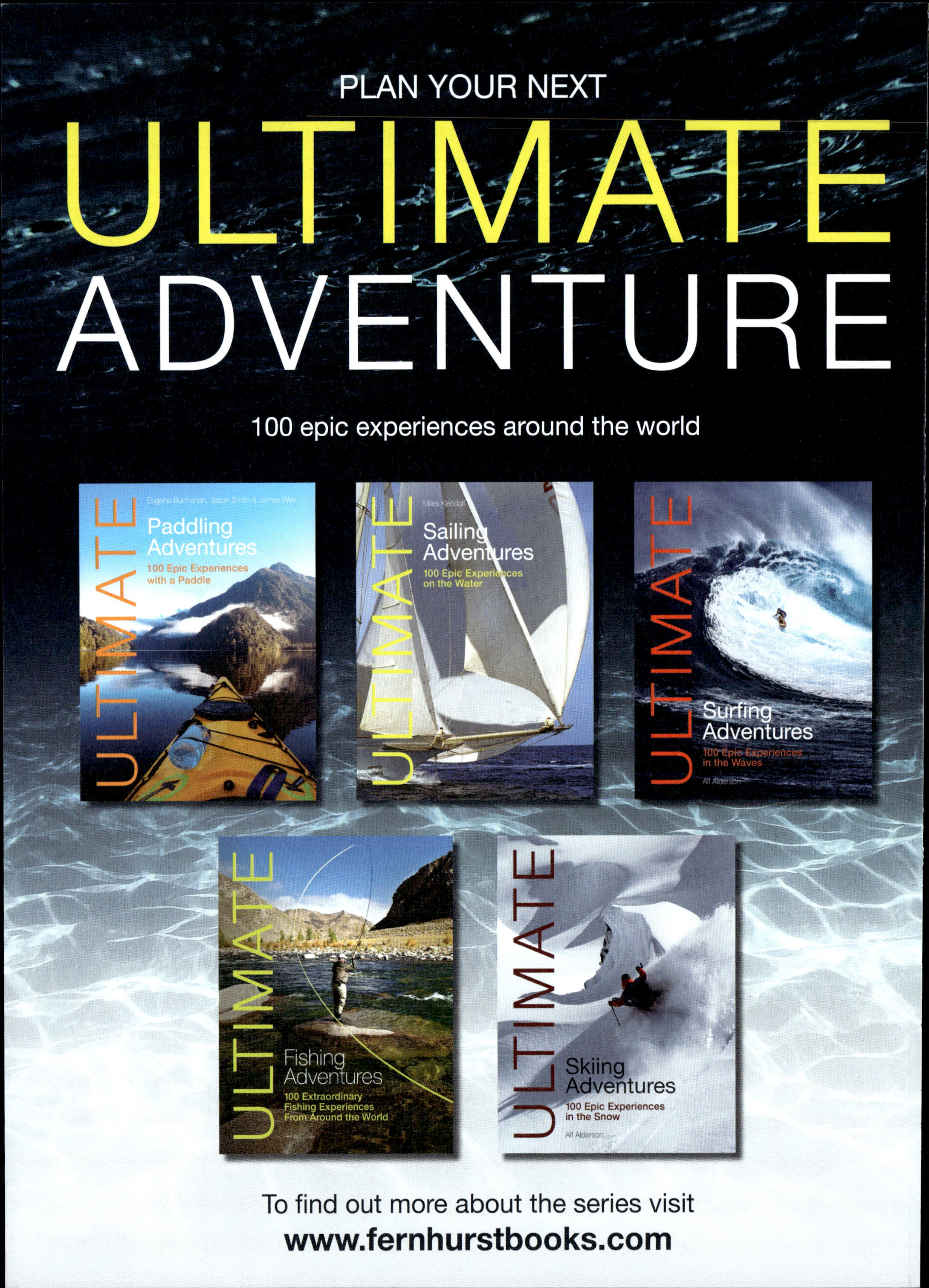

PLAN YOUR NEXT
ULTIMATE
ADVENTURE
100 epic experiences around the world
ULTIMATE
Paddling Adventures
100 Epic Experiences with a Paddle
ULTIMATE
Miles Kendall
Sailing Adventures
100 Epic Experiences on the Water
ULTIMATE
Surfing Adventures
100 Epic Experiences in the Waves
Alf Alderson
ULTIMATE
Fishing Adventures
100 Extraordinary Fishing Experiences From Around the World
ULTIMATE
Skiing Adventures
100 Epic Experiences in the Snow
Alf Alderson
To find out more about the series visit
www.fernhurstbooks.com